PRAISE FOR

THE ATOMIC BAZAAR

"[Langewiesche] insightfully examines the perils created by [the] leveling of the global playing field . . . Buried within [his] grim assessment is a . . . kind of optimism, bolstered by the tenacious reporting for which this author is well known."
—Janet Maslin, *The New York Times*

"This is an important book—an urgent book . . . Chilling."
—Steve Weinberg, *The Christian Science Monitor*

"*The Atomic Bazaar* is an excellent introduction to this most discomfiting topic. It is remarkably comprehensive . . . Through detailed reporting—from closed nuclear cities in the southern Urals to smuggler trails in Kurdistan—the author corrects many popular misunderstandings about the nuclear business."
—*The Economist*

"William Langewiesche . . . is the best reporter most folks have never heard of . . . In his precise, clear, muddy-boots-on-the-ground style, Langewiesche explains the complex problem of nuclear proliferation."   —Kevin Horrigan, *St. Louis Post-Dispatch*

"A straightforward, elegantly concise narrative . . . Eye-opening . . . Langewiesche is an immensely talented and determined journalist . . . Essential reading."   —Chuck Leddy, *Hartford Courant*

"Readers of *The Atomic Bazaar* will come away with a new understanding of nuclear proliferation. And for those who enjoy reading espionage, political science and nuclear weapons instructional manuals, this book is the bomb."
—Richard Horan, *The Atlanta Journal-Constitution*

"In *The Atomic Bazaar*, Langewiesche—one of this country's top investigative journalists—offers a primer on the nuclear tensions in today's headlines." —*Discover*

"This veteran journalist dramatically lays out a worrisome tale of a game with new rules. While thoroughly grounded in complex matters of science and technology, *The Atomic Bazaar* is compelling and reads more like a political thriller . . . Langewiesche is a clear-eyed reporter and *The Atomic Bazaar* is an eye-opener." —Martin Zimmerman, *The San Diego Union-Tribune*

"Beautifully written . . . William Langeweische is a sublime writer. Despite his best efforts, nobody sane could come away from this book unfrightened . . . Everyone should read this book . . . [Langewiesche] is the best guide we have to our unclear nuclear zone." —Christopher Bray, *New Statesman*

"Intrepid and electrifying . . . Langewiesche's bracing exposé of nuclear criminality blasts away the ubiquitous misinformation usually attendant on this alarming subject." —Donna Seaman, *Booklist*

"[Langewiesche's] blunt summary of this sorry history pulls no punches and offers very little consolation . . . Essential reading." —*Kirkus Reviews* (starred review)

"One-stop shopping for the future where nations you fear will have weapons you dread. And there is little you can do about it except to read this excellent book and face the facts your government keeps secret and your leaders fail to comprehend." —Charles Bowden, author of *Blood Orchid: An Unnatural History of America*

Greg Martin

WILLIAM LANGEWIESCHE

THE ATOMIC BAZAAR

William Langewiesche is the author of five previous books, *Cutting for Sign*, *Sahara Unveiled*, *Inside the Sky*, *American Ground*, and *The Outlaw Sea*. He is currently International Correspondent for *Vanity Fair*, and was for years a national correspondent for *The Atlantic Monthly*, where this book originated.

THE ATOMIC BAZAAR

DISPATCHES FROM THE UNDERGROUND

WORLD OF NUCLEAR TRAFFICKING

WILLIAM LANGEWIESCHE

FARRAR, STRAUS AND GIROUX   NEW YORK

Farrar, Straus and Giroux
18 West 18th Street, New York 10011

Grateful acknowledgment is made to *The Atlantic Monthly*,
where this book originated.

"Customs Officials Say Iraq Is Shopping for Centrifuge U Enrichment Hardware,"
by Mark Hibbs, reprinted by permission of *NuclearFuel*, a Platts publication.

Library of Congress Cataloging-in-Publication Data
Langewiesche, William.
    The atomic bazaar : dispatches from the underground world of nuclear
trafficking / William Langewiesche. — 1st paperback ed.
        p.   cm.
    ISBN-13: 978-0-374-53132-4 (pbk. : alk. paper)
    ISBN-10: 0-374-53132-3 (pbk. : alk. paper)
    1. Nuclear weapons.   2. Nuclear weapons—Pakistan.   3. Nuclear
nonproliferation.   4. World politics—21st century.   I. Title.

U264.L365 2008
355.02'17095491—dc22

                                                          2007047624

Designed by Jonathan D. Lippincott

www.fsgbooks.com

1   3   5   7   9   10   8   6   4   2

CONTENTS

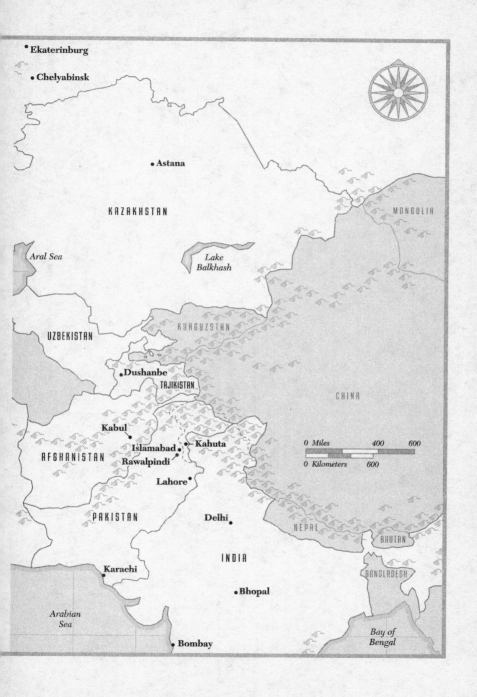

THE ATOMIC BAZAAR

ONE

THE VANGUARD OF THE POOR

Hiroshima was destroyed in a flash by a bomb dropped from a propeller-driven B-29 of the U.S. Army Air Corps, on the warm morning of Monday, August 6, 1945. The bomb was not chemical, as bombs until then had been, but atomic, designed to release the energies that Einstein had described. It was a simple cannon-type device of the sort that today any number of people could build in a garage. It was bulbous and black, about ten feet long, and weighed ninety-seven hundred pounds. It fell nose-down for forty-three seconds and, for maximum effect, never hit the ground. One thousand nine hundred feet above the city it fired a dull gray plug of highly enriched uranium down a steel tube into a receiving lump of the same refined material, creating a combined uranium mass of 133 pounds. In relation to its surface area, that mass was more than enough to achieve "criticality" and allow for an uncontrollable chain of fission reactions, during which subatomic particles called neutrons collided with uranium nuclei, releasing further neutrons, which collided with other nuclei, in a blossoming process of self-destruction. The reactions could be sustained for just a millisecond, and they fully

exploited less than two pounds of the uranium atoms before the
resulting heat forced a halt to the process through expansion.
Uranium is one of the heaviest elements on earth, almost twice
as heavy as lead, and two pounds of it amounts to only about
three tablespoonfuls. Nonetheless the release of energy over
Hiroshima yielded a force equivalent to fifteen thousand tons
(fifteen kilotons) of TNT, achieved temperatures higher than the
sun's, and emitted light-speed pulses of lethal radiation. More
than 150,000 people died.

Their executioner was an ordinary pilot named Paul Tibbets,
who was twenty-nine then and is still alive now, in Ohio. He neither abhorred nor enjoyed the kill: he was a flight technician, removed from the slaughter by altitude and speed, and coddled
by a pressurized, well-heated cockpit. That morning the sky was
quiet, with no sign of enemy opposition. The B-29 cruised thirty-
one thousand feet above the city in smooth air. It lurched and
nosed upward when the bomb fell clear. Tibbets banked steeply
to get away and turned the airplane's tail on the destruction.
When the bomb ignited, now far behind and below, it lit the sky
with the prettiest blues and pinks that Tibbets had ever seen.
The first shock wave came shimmering through the atmosphere
and overtook the airplane from behind, causing a sharp bump
measured at 2.5 g's by a cockpit accelerometer. The bump felt
about like the near miss of an antiaircraft burst, or the jolt of
crossing a pothole in a jeep. A second shock wave then hit, but it
was a reflection off the ground, like an echo of the first, and
therefore even less intense. Tibbets tasted the fillings in his
teeth. He saw the cloud rising over Hiroshima, and, as must be
expected, he felt no regrets.

Still, Hiroshima was not good for him. Though he became a
brigadier general in the U.S. Air Force, and later the chairman of

an executive-jet company, he suffered from the stigma of having killed so many, and he grew bitter about any implication that what he had done was wrong. It was unrealistic and probably unfair to expect him to repent, but over the decades American elites did just that, having first required him to drop the bomb. In his retirement he took to traveling around the country giving talks to war buffs and like-minded reactionaries. He showed up at air shows, I suppose to shake hands. In the 1990s, he waded angrily into a minor controversy about the Smithsonian's display of the forward section of his airplane, the _Enola Gay_, and accused the elites of manipulating public opinion for their self-interest. He said he was a pilot and soldier, and by implication a simple man. He sold trinkets on the Internet, including, for $500, a beautifully rendered one-twelfth-scale atomic-bomb model mounted on a (solid, not veneer) mahogany base, and accompanied by an autographed data plate. For those with smaller budgets, he offered a sheet of thirty-six commemorative stamps picturing a B-29 soaring beyond a mushroom cloud, with excellent detail of boiling smoke on the ground. Tibbets may have been bullheaded, but at least he was consistent. When the writer Studs Terkel interviewed him in 2002, eleven months after the September 11 attacks, he did not bemoan the sadness of war or ruminate on the difficulty of facing a stateless foe, but opted true to form for a nuclear response. Against Kabul? Cairo? Mecca? He said, "You're gonna kill innocent people at the same time, but we've never fought a damn war anywhere in the world where they [he meant _we_] didn't kill innocent people. If the newspapers would just cut out the shit: 'You've killed so many civilians!' That's their tough luck for being there."

Tibbets spoke from experience, and in a narrow sense he was right: it was indeed just tough luck for all the innocents who died under his wings in 1945. Those people, however, did not constitute collateral casualties—any more than the victims in the World Trade Center did. In fact Hiroshima had been chosen primarily as a civilian target and had in part been exempted from conventional firebombing to preserve it for the most dramatic possible demonstration of a nuclear strike. Three days later, the city of Nagasaki was hit by an even more powerful device—a sophisticated implosion-type bomb built around a softball-sized sphere of plutonium, which crossed the weight-to-surface-area threshold of "criticality" when it was symmetrically compressed by carefully arrayed explosives. A twenty-two-kiloton blast resulted. Though much of the city was shielded by hills, about seventy thousand people died. Quibblers claim that a demonstration offshore, or even above Tokyo harbor, might have induced the Japanese to surrender with less loss of life—and that if not, another bomb was ready. But the intent was to terrorize a nation to the maximum extent, and there is nothing like nuking civilians to achieve that effect.

It's too bad, but such is the world we live in. And cities are soft targets. More accurately, they are flammable, dense, and brittle. This goes for New York, with all its high-quality concrete and steel, and even more for the new urban conglomerations of Asia. Beyond this there are significant differences in the dynamics of nuclear blasts, dependent largely on the size of the explosion and the altitude at which it takes place. A Hiroshima-sized terrorist attack at street level in Times Square would shatter midtown Manhattan and raise a cloud of radioactive debris which would settle downwind, lethally, perhaps across Queens. By comparison a North Korean airburst of the same size a half mile above Seoul would cause still larger destruction, but result in less radioactive fallout. These variations, however, become mere details when they are measured against the common result: any city hit by a nuclear bomb will fall badly apart. And a Hiroshima-sized device now lies well within the capacities of any number of nations.

When such a device ignites, the nuclear chain reaction endures for a millionth of a second. During that interval, a lethal burst of neutron particles shoots outward, penetrating walls and people in the immediate vicinity, but losing energy within a few hundred yards, as the neutrons collide with the air. Simultaneously, and for seconds afterward, a pulse of electromagnetic gamma rays, similar to light but far more powerful, flows at dangerous levels through the city to a distance of about two miles. All this would be serious enough, but it is just the start. Even in combination, these two forms of radiation (known as the initial radiation) account for only about 5 percent of the energy released by the bomb. Another 10 percent is released well after ignition, by the radioactive residue that may fall to the ground or go drifting off through the atmosphere. But all the rest of the bomb's energy—85 percent of the yield—is transformed into airblast and heat. Nuclear bombs of the Hiroshima size destroy cities by smashing and burning them down.

These primitive effects kill almost everyone who would otherwise be dying quickly of acute radiation, then spread out to kill many more. They begin within less than a millionth of a second, when the fission process releases massive amounts of invisible X-rays, which at low altitude are absorbed by the air within a few feet. The resulting heat, rising to tens of millions of degrees, raises the pressures within the vaporizing weapon to several million times that of the surrounding atmosphere. Still within the first millionth of a second, an ultrabright fireball forms, consisting of gasified weapons residues and air. The fireball brutally expands and simultaneously rises. Within three seconds of a twenty-kiloton explosion, it reaches its maximum size, about 1,500 feet across. If it touches the ground (whether because the ignition point was on a street, or at less than 750 feet overhead), it vaporizes the earth and all structures that it encounters and begins to loft large quantities of dirt and debris into a violently rising, intensely radioactive column.

Rising in that column along with all the ash and earth are hundreds of by-products of the fission, many of which are radioactive, but a good number of which decay so rapidly that they reach the end of their radioactive lives before they settle again to the ground. Rapid decay is a common characteristic of the most radioactive fission by-products. Seven hours after ignition, the emissions of the fallout are approximately one-tenth as strong as at the one-hour mark; after two days, the radioactivity has bled away to merely one-hundredth of the same one-hour value. Such decay accounts for the fact that people living downwind under even the thickest fallout will probably be able to escape safely (though they may suffer medical consequences in the long run), if only they can avoid exposure for the first few hours following the blast. Avoidance is difficult for those not specially prepared to protect themselves, and as a result many people will grow sick or die from the fallout. But residual radioactivity turns out not to be the greatest danger of a twenty-kiloton bomb.

So back to the first small fraction of a second. As the fireball grows, it reradiates some of the energy in the form of two thermal pulses. The mechanisms behind these pulses have to do with the intense temperatures and internal dynamics of the nuclear fireball, the understanding of which must surely rank among the most coolly analytical of practical human knowledge. The first pulse is short and weak and accounts for only 1 percent of the fireball's thermal radiation. It consists of ultraviolet waves, and at a short distance may sunburn human skin but poses no serious danger except for damage to the eyes of the few people who happen to have been focusing in exactly the wrong direction at exactly the wrong time. By contrast the second pulse is massive, accounting for all the rest of the fireball's thermal radiation, and continuing for an eternity—perhaps two seconds. It consists primarily of visible light and infrared emissions and, in a nuclear explosion even of this relatively modest size, is capable not only of burning eyes and skin, but of igniting combustible materials and wooden structures as far as a mile ahead of the fireball's front.

Then comes the blast. It begins as a shock wave at the fireball's birth and propagates outward initially at supersonic speeds. Within the first tenth of a second it overtakes the now slowing expansion of the fireball and bursts through the fireball's surface. Sharply pressurizing and heating the atmosphere, the shock front slows to the speed of sound and continues outward, with enormous destructive power. If the bomb was exploded in the air, there are actually two shock waves, the primary one, then a reflection off the ground. Roughly one and a quarter seconds after detonation, and a third of a mile away from the ignition point, the reflection catches up to the leading shock wave and merges with it into a single vertical front. If the bomb was exploded on the street, as it might be, say, in New York, there is no reflective wave, and the shock front travels from the very start as one. Either way the effects are about the same. Though people can withstand greater pressure spikes than the shock wave delivers, the structures they inhabit cannot. Three seconds after detonation, the shock wave is just under a mile from the ignition point and, in the case of a twenty-kiloton bomb, is breaking structures with a hammer blow of air pressure, and then tearing them apart with outflowing winds of 180 miles an hour. The violence is such that fires that may have been ignited by the thermal pulse are snuffed out. Ten seconds after detonation, the shock wave has moved two and a half miles out and has weakened significantly, but is still capable of making projectiles of glass, tearing doors from their frames, and collapsing some concrete or cinder-block walls.

There is a moment of calm.

The fireball is no longer visible, but it is still extremely hot, and it is vigorously rising into the atmosphere. A result of its rise, and of a partial vacuum that has just been formed by the displacement of air, the winds now reverse and begin to flow back toward the epicenter at speeds up to two hundred miles an hour, ripping apart damaged structures that have somehow so far remained standing. These "afterwinds" raise dirt and debris into the base of the telltale mushroom cloud now beginning to form. The broken city lies like kindling, and whether because of electrical shorts or gas pilot lights, it begins to burn. Depending on conditions, the fires may spread and join, to create the sort of firestorm that was seen in Hiroshima, though not Nagasaki. Either way, the destruction of the city is complete, and in overfilled places such as New York or Seoul—or Mumbai—it is likely that several hundred thousand people have lost their lives.

From the start in the 1940s, the physicists who developed these devices understood the potential for physical miniaturization and a simultaneous escalation in explosive yields past the twenty-two kilotons of Nagasaki, and indeed past a thousand kilotons, into the multimegaton range—the realm, when multiplied, of global suicide. Moreover they realized that the science involved, however mysterious it seemed to laymen, had already devolved into mere problems of engineering, the knowledge of which could not be contained. Within a few years humanity would face the risk of annihilation—an objective reality that compelled those who understood it best to go public with the facts. In the months following the Japanese surrender, a group of the men responsible for producing the bomb—including Albert Einstein, Robert Oppenheimer, Niels Bohr, Leo Szilard, and others—created the Federation of American (Atomic) Scientists (FAS) to educate U.S. political leaders and the American public about the realities of nuclear weapons. Washington at the time harbored the illusion that America possessed a great secret and could keep the bomb for itself to drop or not on others. The founders of the FAS disagreed. They argued that with the destruction of Hiroshima the only two significant questions had emphatically been answered: could a practical and deliverable device actually be built, and if so would it be put to use? The attempt to go through with the construction of an atomic bomb—to do it for real, and particularly to manufacture the few hundred pounds of bomb-grade fuel that were necessary—had amounted to a national-scale gamble that only the United States could have risked during war in advance of affirmative answers to those questions. But now that Hiroshima had demonstrated the practicality of the venture, the calculation had changed, and it was obvious that other nations could make the investment in full certainty of the return. Some would be friends of the United States, and some would be enemies. Any number of physicists and engineers worldwide were capable of guiding them through the process. The FAS warned the American people in stark and simple terms. In essence they said that the whole world would soon be nuclear-armed. They said, there is no secret here, and there is also no defense. The nuclear age is upon us, and it cannot be undone.

Some of the solutions they proposed may now seem quaint. Albert Einstein, for instance, called for the creation of an enlightened global government, complete with the integration of formerly hostile military staffs, and the voluntary dismantling of sovereign states. But the founders of the FAS were not naive so much as desperate and brave. In essence they said, if you knew what we know about these devices, you would agree that at any price the practice of war must stop. It was a rare call for radical change by men at the top of their game, and a measure of the collective dread.

Indeed there was no secret. The spread of nuclear weapons to competing states was accelerated by espionage, but by no means dependent upon it. Each of the new nuclear powers was capable on its own of building the bomb—just as the American scientists had warned. And yet events turned out to be difficult to predict, even for such thinkers as these. Simply put, after more than six decades the predicted apocalypse has not yet occurred, and a nuclear peace has endured for all the wrong reasons—an unenlightened standoff between the nuclear powers, each of them restrained from taking the first shot not by moral qualms but by the certainty of a devastating response. The very lack of defense that so worried the scientists in 1945 turned out to *be* the defense, though treacherous because it required mutual escalation. But these are latter-day corrections to the concerns of enormously competent men, whose basic message remains valid today. Even after sixty years of success, the nuclear standoff is still a temporary answer to a permanent threat. Furthermore, detailed knowledge of nuclear bomb-making has fully escaped into the public domain, placing nuclear arsenals within the reach of almost any nation. Once countries make that choice, their rivals will hear the same call. The United States, Russia, Britain, France, China, Israel, South Africa, India, Pakistan, North Korea, and soon perhaps Iran. At least twenty other countries are in position to proceed. In the long run it hardly matters that some countries have been persuaded to abandon their nuclear ambitions, and that one—South Africa—has laid down its arms. Nuclear proliferation moves in fits and starts and sometimes slips backward, but incrementally proceeds. Diplomacy may help to slow the spread, but it can no more stop the process than it can reverse the progression of time. The nuclearization of the world has become the human condition, and it cannot be changed. Fear of it becomes dangerous when it detracts from realistic assessments of the terrain. The risk of an all-out exchange has been reduced since the end of the Cold War, but by no means can it be ignored. At the same time, and as a result of the Soviet Union's demise, the world has become a more fractured and complex place, where nuclear weapons have even wider utility than before, and new nuclear players are emerging to challenge the rules of the game.

Recently in Moscow I spoke to an experienced Cold War hand who had navigated through the collapse of the Soviet Union and had emerged high in the nuclear bureaucracy of the newly entrepreneurial Russia. In his corduroy suit, with his untrimmed eyebrows and heavy, sometimes glowering face, he bore traces of the past, but mentally he was a man of the times. He kept poking his finger at me, and accusing Americans of losing perspective over a nuclear Iran. He wanted to do nuclear business with Iran, in electric-power generation. He wanted to do nuclear business with all sorts of countries. He claimed that with one Russian submarine reactor fueled by highly enriched uranium he could light up all sorts of cities. He meant with electricity. He proposed a scheme to mount such reactors on ocean barges to be pushed to places like Indonesia, then pulled away whenever the natives run amok. This way he could keep his uranium from fueling native bombs. He did not deny the incentives for lesser nations to acquire nuclear devices, but he thought he could handle them, or perhaps he didn't care.

We talked about history. Speaking of the main international agreement intended to limit the spread of nuclear weapons, he said, "The Nuclear Non-Proliferation Treaty was the child of Russia and the United States. And this child was raised to fight against other countries, to resist the threat of proliferation. We're talking about the 1970s now. No one thought that proliferation could come from Arab countries, from Africa, from South America. The treaty was aimed at West Germany, at Japan. It was aimed at dissuading the developed countries from acquiring nuclear weapons—and it worked because they accepted the U.S. and Soviet nuclear umbrellas."

I thought he was bullying the history a bit, but making an important point. The Nuclear Non-Proliferation Treaty, or NPT, was an effort to preserve the exclusivity of a weapons club whose membership consisted originally of only five: Britain, China, France, the Soviet Union, and the United States. To other countries the treaty promised assistance with nuclear research and power generation in return for commitments to abstain from nuclear arms. The arrangement cannot be said to have "worked," as the Russian claimed, but it did help to slow things down. More important, however, and independent of the treaty, were the Cold

War alliances that, by offering retaliatory guarantees, eliminated the need for independent nuclear-defense capabilities in those nations willing or forced to choose sides. Sweden abandoned its nuclear-weapons program, as did Taiwan. Moreover it was not by chance that the first successful newcomers beyond the original Club of Five were South Africa and Israel, which were maverick states, and India, which was formally unaligned. But things have changed. The remnant alliances of the Cold War have lost much of their power, and they now offer poor assurance of a nuclear response: the umbrella has frayed or, in many cases, entirely gone away. Simply put, large parts of the world are exposed once again to the universal appeal of atomic bombs—the fast-track, nation-equalizing, don't-tread-on-me, flat-out-awesome destructive power that independent arsenals can provide.

In 1946 Robert Oppenheimer sketched our times clearly, not by making predictions about it, but by describing the technology then at hand. In an essay entitled "The New Weapon," he wrote, "Atomic explosives vastly increase the power of destruction per dollar spent, per man-hour invested; they profoundly upset the precarious balance between the effort necessary to destroy, and the extent of the destruction." Elaborating, he wrote, "None of the uncertainties can becloud the fact it will cost enormously less to destroy a square mile with atomic weapons than with any weapons hitherto known to warfare. My own estimate is that the advent of such weapons will reduce the cost, certainly by more than a factor of ten, more probably by a factor of a hundred. In this respect only biological warfare would seem to offer competition for the evil that a dollar can do."

In Moscow, the Russian continued in the same vein. Speaking first of the nuclear arms race between the Soviet Union and the United States, he said, "We understood that these weapons could never be used, paradoxically because both sides had so many. For us the stockpiles were not wealth. They became a burden that our countries had to bear. But at the same time, globally, nuclear technology was growing cheaper and more efficient, and it was becoming an option for many countries." He meant the technology both of electric-power generation and of bombs, which is nearly the same. He said, "Undeveloped countries."

I said, "Like Iran."

He batted this away. "Many different countries. Nuclear-weapons technology has become a useful tool *especially* for the weak. It allows them to satisfy their ambitions without much expense. If they want to intimidate others, to be respected by others, this is now the easiest way to do it. Just produce nuclear weapons. The technology has become so simple that there are no technical barriers, and no barriers to the flow of information, that can prevent it. This is a reality you Americans need to understand."

I said, "Clearly."

He said, "Once a country has made the political decision to become a nuclear-weapons power, it will become one regardless of international sanctions or incentives. You needn't be rich. You needn't be technically developed. You can be Pakistan, Libya, North Korea, Iran. You can be . . ."

You can be South Korea, Turkey, Egypt, Syria, Algeria, South Africa again, Brazil—the list of aspirants, both real and potential, is long.

But he was searching for a country even more absurd in his estimation. He said, "You can be Hungary."

Then he said, "At some point this change occurred. The great powers were stuck with arsenals they could not use, and nuclear weapons became the weapons of the poor."

TWO

NUKES WITHOUT NATIONS

From a lofty view there is justice in a world where the weak become stronger, and the strong have no choice but to accommodate the gain. Practically speaking, however, the poor, for a host of reasons, are more likely to use their nuclear weapons than the great powers have been, at least since the United States terrorized Japan. At the extreme is the possibility, entirely real, that one or two nuclear weapons will pass into the hands of the new stateless guerrillas, the jihadists, who offer none of the retaliatory targets that have so far underlain the nuclear peace—no permanent infrastructure to protect, no capital city, and indeed no country called home. The danger first arose in the chaos of post-Soviet Russia in the 1990s, and it took full form after the September 11 attacks of 2001. The U.S. government's subsequent manipulation of the fear is deplorable and tragic: far better to accept the risk soberly, and to examine it realistically, than to dash around making blind wars, limiting liberties and commerce, and generally self-destructing in advance. Nonetheless the fact remains: with so little to lose from nuclear retaliation, and in need of ever more dramatic acts in their war against the West, these jihadists are the people who would not hesitate to detonate a nuclear device.

Of course they may also pursue their war in other spectacular ways, including small-scale bombings, poison-gas assaults in enclosed public spaces, and more difficult biological attacks. Within the nominally nuclear realm, they may choose to set off "dirty bombs," which would use conventional explosives not to induce a fission reaction, but to scatter ordinary, detectable radioactive materials through a few city blocks, causing public hysteria—all the more so in societies where even outdoor tobacco smoke is called a threat. Dirty bombs would be mere nuisance bombs if people would keep their calm. But of course people will not. The potential effectiveness of such a device was loudly signaled by the clamor about dangerous dust around the World Trade Center site, and it was reinforced more recently by the outraged reaction to an attempt by a U.S. agency to raise the acceptable threshold of radiation for reinhabiting an area after a dirty-bomb attack. The outrage must have been noticed by the people who count. Furthermore they must know that even just in the United States there are large quantities of nonfissionable but highly radioactive materials contained within machines, primarily in hospitals and at industrial sites, and that the machines, because they are expensive, are sometimes stolen for resale. In fact in the United States alone there are hundreds of thefts of radioactive material every year. As to why no dirty bomb has yet been assembled and used, analysts provide earnest explanations, but largely to avoid throwing up their hands in wonder.

In any event a true atomic bomb—a fission device such as the one that destroyed Hiroshima—is an entirely different weapon, far more difficult to obtain or build, but hugely more effective if used. Beyond the immediate havoc that would be caused by the blast, the ongoing reactions to the 9/11 attacks offer the merest indication of the massive self-devouring that would subsequently occur. In Western capitals today there are quiet people, serious people, who, while recognizing the low probability of such an attack, nonetheless worry that the successful use of just a single atomic bomb could bring the established order to its knees—or lay it out flat.

If you were a terrorist intent on carrying out a nuclear strike, you could not count on acquiring an existing device. These are held as critical national assets in fortified facilities guarded by elite troops, and they would be extremely difficult to get at, or to buy. Some reports suggest the contrary, particularly because of rumors about the penetration of organized crime into the Russian nuclear forces, and about portable satchel nukes, or "suitcase bombs," which are said to have been built for the KGB in the late 1970s and 1980s, and then lost into the global black market following the Soviet breakup a few years later. The existence of suitcase bombs has never been proved, however, and there has never been a single verified case, anywhere, of the theft of any sort of nuclear weapon. Thefts may nonetheless have occurred, particularly during the chaos of the mid-1990s, but nuclear weapons require regular maintenance, and any of them still lingering on the market today would likely by now have become duds. Conversely, because these time limitations are well-known, the very lack of a terrorist nuclear strike thus far hints that nothing useful was stolen in the first place. Either way, even if the seller could provide a functioning device, nuclear weapons in Russia and other advanced states are protected by electronic locks that would defeat almost any attempt to trigger an explosion. Of course you could look to countries where less rigorous safe-guards are in place, but no government handles its nuclear arse-nal loosely or would dare to create the impression that it is using surrogates to fight its nuclear wars. Even the military leaders of Pakistan, who have repeatedly demonstrated their willingness to sell nuclear-weapons technology abroad, would balk at allowing a constructed bomb to escape—if only because of the certainty that after the blast, the trail would be backtracked, and they would be held to account. The same concerns will almost cer-tainly now constrain North Korea and Iran.

If you were a terrorist, all this might give you pause to take your bearings. You would need to distinguish between your own needs as a stateless fighter, and those of conventional govern-mental proliferators. Even the youngest nuclear-weapons states—such as Pakistan or North Korea—have little use for just one or two bombs. To assume a convincing posture of counterstrike and deterrence, or simply to exhibit nuclear muscle, they require a significant arsenal that can be renewed and improved and grown across time. This in turn requires that they build large-scale industrial facilities to produce warhead fuel, which cannot be purchased in sufficient quantity on the international black market to sustain a nuclear-weapons production line. Manufac-turing high-quality fuel is still the most difficult and important part of any nuclear program. It is something that a stateless group simply cannot do.

But this is not necessarily a problem. Indeed, giving up on the manufacture of fuel would largely remove you from the reach of the NPT and other nonproliferation efforts, which focus on inter-rupting the spread of weapons at that stage. Furthermore, an ex-cess of weapons-ready fissile material is already stockpiled in the world today, of which you require only a small amount. Keep in mind that unlike governments with territory to protect, you can attack with near impunity and accomplish your purposes with merely one or two garage-made bombs. Surely you can find a way to buy or steal the necessary fuel.

It would be helpful at this early point to consider exactly what kind of fuel to pursue. For ordinary fission bombs, there are really only two choices—either plutonium or highly enriched uranium. Plutonium is a man-made element produced by uranium reactors, from which it emerges initially mixed in with the other radioactive waste, but is separable through chemical processes. There are several forms of it, including one purpose-made for bombs. Armies favor plutonium because it is highly fissionable and can be made to go critical in small quantities, thereby lending itself to the miniaturization of weapons. Miniaturization has obvious attractions, but it requires a level of engineering sophistication, related mostly to the efficiency of nuclear chain reactions, that lies beyond the capabilities of a small terrorist team. And miniaturization is not that important for the purposes at hand. You can hit New York or London well enough with a car-sized device locked into a shipping container or loaded into a private airplane behind a couple of dedicated pilots. Furthermore, ignoring the question of size, plutonium has a couple of negatives for an operation such as yours. For technical reasons it is not suited for use in a basic cannon-type bomb and demands instead the explosive symmetry of a Nagasaki-style implosion device. Building an implosion device would introduce complexities you would be better off avoiding, particularly without a place and the time to test the design. And plutonium is difficult to handle—sufficiently radioactive to require shielding, awkward to transport without setting off radiation detectors, and extremely dangerous even in minute quantities if it is breathed in, swallowed, or ab-

sorbed into the body through a cut or open wound. Plenty of
people in this world would willingly die for the chance to nuke
the United States, but within the limited pool of technicians who
might join your effort, it would be impractical to expect so much.
Specialists I have spoken to widely agree. Plutonium might work
as the pollutant spread by a dirty bomb, but for the purposes of a
simple fission device, plutonium is out.

The alternative is highly enriched uranium, or HEU, containing more than 90 percent of the fissionable isotope, U-235. Oper-
ationally it is wonderful stuff—the perfect fuel for a garage-made
bomb. During processing, it takes the form of an invisible gas, a
liquid, a powder, and finally a dull gray metal that is cool and dry
to the touch. It has approximately the toxicity of lead and would
sicken shop workers who swallowed traces of it or breathed in its
dust, but otherwise it is not immediately dangerous and, indeed,
is so mildly radioactive that it can be picked up with bare hands,
transported in a backpack, and, when lightly shielded, taken past
most radiation monitors without setting off alarms. As one physicist suggested to me, in small masses HEU is so benign that
you could sleep with it under your pillow if you so desired. He
warned me that you could not, however, just casually pile it
up. The reason is that the atoms of U-235 occasionally and spontaneously split apart, and in doing so they fire off neutrons, which
within a sufficient mass of material could split enough other
atoms to cause a blossoming chain reaction. Such a reaction
would not amount to a military-style nuclear explosion, but it
could certainly release enough energy to take out a few city
blocks.

The physicist had an office near the White House in Washington, D.C. I asked him if he wasn't concerned about giving information to terrorists who could strike his neighbors, himself, or

his wife. He summoned his patience visibly and said, to paraphrase it, This is Boy Scout Nuclear Merit Badge stuff. We continued our discussion. He said that for any given shape (a sphere being optimal) the critical mass of uranium is inversely proportional to the level of enrichment. At the low end of HEU, which is considered to be 20 percent enrichment, nearly a ton would have to be combined before a stockpile could spontaneously ignite. At the high end, which is the "weapons-grade" enrichment of 90 percent or greater, less than one hundred pounds could do the trick.

I mentioned that at whatever level of enrichment, in whatever form, the HEU that a terrorist could acquire would by definition be made of units each consisting of less than a critical mass. I asked the physicist to imagine that a terrorist had acquired two bricks of weapons-grade HEU, each weighing fifty pounds: how far apart would he have to keep them? The physicist suggested that a yard would be enough. I had just arrived in Washington from remote mountains along the Turkish border with Iran, where every night hundreds of packhorses are led across the line by Kurdish smugglers, bringing in cheap fuel for Turkish cars and Central Asian opium for the European heroin market. This is the Silk Road revived, and one of the prime potential routes for the movement of stolen uranium. With the practicalities in mind, I told the physicist I assumed from his measure that a person could sling the two bricks on either side of a single saddle, for balance.

He said, "One on each side should be all right—" He hesitated. "But what is the moderating effect of a horse?"

I had no idea.

He pointed out that horses are made mostly of water, and that water, by slowing neutrons down, actually decreases the mass re-

quired for a chain reaction. So this is tricky stuff. He said, "Look,
if someone's smart enough to have snuck in and gotten ahold of
these two ingots of metal, he'll be smart enough to negotiate for
a second horse."

But you would probably rather not have to sneak into anywhere
or negotiate for transport or spend cold nights squatting with
peasants and dodging border patrols in the darkness of the
mountains. Every move in this venture, every elaboration, increases the chance for something to go wrong. Furthermore, to
judge from the reports that have been written about a global
black market in fissile materials, it might be possible to sit on the
periphery—preferably in the lovely city of Istanbul—and with
relatively little risk allow the uranium to come to you.

It is difficult to get a clear picture here. Since the breakup
of the Soviet Union, the International Atomic Energy Agency
(IAEA) has reported seventeen officially declared cases of trafficking in plutonium or HEU, generally Russian-made. This is
certainly an undercount, though perhaps by a smaller factor than
is usually said. The activity was strongest in the early and mid-
1990s, when it seemed to be directed toward a half-imagined
network of arms dealers in Central and Western Europe. The
reported incidents then tapered off for a few years, but they
resumed in 1998 and have continued intermittently ever since.
At the same time there seems to have been a shift in the smuggling routes, away from Western Europe, and across the southern Caucasus (Georgia, Azerbaijan, Armenia, perhaps Iran) into
Turkey. Turkey is the world's grand bazaar, and given its geo-
graphic position overlooking the Middle East, it is hardly surprising that in recent years people have gone there looking to sell

their nuclear goods. A University of Salzburg database (formerly run by Stanford) that purports to track such activity globally since 1993 lists at least twenty incidents in the vicinity of Istanbul alone. But by including intercepts of all sorts of nuclear materials, that database (like most other treatments in this business) overstates the market's ability to answer a bomb-maker's needs. Though militaries can do with less, as a bomb-building neophyte you would require at least one hundred pounds of HEU enriched to 90 percent or better. It's true that you could perhaps use material enriched to as little as 60 percent, but you would need a correspondingly greater mass to work with; any lesser level of enrichment would simply be no use at all. In fact the marketplace—whether in Istanbul or elsewhere—seems never to have produced the materials that would be required. The closest instance I found in the record dates from 1998, when agents from the Russian Federal Security Bureau (the former KGB, now called the FSB) arrested nuclear workers who were plotting to steal forty pounds of HEU from one of the secret cities near Chelyabinsk, just east of the Urals. The enrichment level was never made public—an omission hinting that the uranium may well have been weapons grade. But even then at best it was less than half of what a terrorist would need.

Of course we don't know what we don't know, as we are repetitively reminded. The other intercepts, however, have been minor affairs of people caught filching or hawking scraps, often of material that doesn't pass even the 20 percent mark. In Ankara I once asked an Israeli who is engaged in this fight on what pretext people try to sell such obvious junk—do they offer it as samples? He said yes, but in every case he knew, these were scams, and usually flimsy ones at that. He dismissed the sellers as small-timers and fools. I asked him if he meant this as a rule. He said it is closer to a natural selection, and he asked me to consider the lopsided character of the marketplace where they work. In the entire world there are perhaps twenty serious customers for a one-off atomic bomb. What sort of man, having acquired some portion of the fuel, would head to Istanbul in the expectation of finding one? What sort of man, having acquired even less, would head there expecting to pull off a nuclear scam? And think about it in actuality. How does he advertise his wares? By word of mouth? To the friend of his friend? And where? On a bench overlooking the Bosporus, in a park, in a bus station café? Is it summer, is it winter, did someone's car break down? These details count. What business is the friend normally in? Why should he be trusted to stay close-lipped and calm? And how would he know the players who matter? What is the connection between racketeers and oil-rich global guerrillas? Is the underworld so tight? Does an underworld as such exist at all? No wonder these traffickers are picked up by the Turks. From distant America—among professors and in the policy circles of Washington—their arrests seem to signal the existence of a dangerous trade, but from up close within the bazaar they mostly just add to a sense that for now even Tel Aviv remains safe. Or so the Israeli told me.

For a serious bomb-builder the reports of "loose nukes" would come to sound like so much background chatter. Despite the risks involved, the fissile material will have to be obtained at the source, and ideally all at once. This will require travel. From the literature, it would appear that one of the first practical challenges is the very extent of available choices. There are for instance more than a hundred civilian research reactors fueled by several tons of weapons-usable highly enriched uranium world-wide, often on university campuses, where security is appropriately light. On further reading, however, it emerges that little of that HEU (and rarely more than a few pounds in one place) is fresh fuel of the sort that would be easy to handle. The rest of it is either cooking inside the reactors or sitting in storage afterward in irradiated forms that to varying degrees have become dangerously radioactive. Some observers suggest that the standards have changed since the attacks of September 11, and that the elegant idea of self-protecting materials no longer applies, because nuclear thieves may be suicidal. This is true, but similar acts of self-sacrifice would also be required of less likely martyrs farther down the line, for instance those working to assemble an irradiated-uranium bomb, and the risk of detection would correspondingly increase. Simply put, from a bomb-builder's perspective it would be best to avoid the really hot material, and all the more so because there are alternatives.

It turns out that the world is rich with fresh, safe, user-friendly HEU—a global accumulation (outside of our collective thirty thousand nuclear warheads) that is dispersed among hundreds of sites and further separated into nicely transportable, necessarily subcritical packages. The combined HEU amounts to over a thousand metric tons, though no one knows just how far over, because governments keep their figures secret and may, in some cases, have only a rough idea of their inventories. A thousand metric tons is 2,205,623 pounds. That represents a lot of fissile material just lying around, when only a hundred pounds are needed. The practical question is how to pick some up. Here again the literature provides some guidance. Although almost all HEU is in some manner guarded, it might nonetheless be acquired in many countries, and probably nowhere better than in Russia.

When post-Soviet Russia came into being, in 1991, it inherited a sprawling state industry that had provided for a full range of nuclear services, including medical science, power generation, and ship propulsion—as well as the world's largest nuclear-weapons arsenal, and almost coincidentally, the world's largest inventory of surplus plutonium and HEU, six hundred metric tons of it, scattered about. The physical plant consisted of several dozen research, production, and storage facilities, and especially of ten fenced and guarded nuclear cities, which housed nearly a million people yet were nominally so secret that they did not appear on maps. Inside the cities people had for decades enjoyed a standard of living well above Soviet average. But by the early 1990s the industry was obsolete, unable to adapt to the new Russian economy, and in steep decline. The buildings stood in disrepair, and morale was low because people were not being paid enough or on time. Worse, the nuclear stockpiles were being neglected. There were stories of guards abandoning their posts to forage for food, and of sheds containing world-ending supplies of HEU protected by padlock only. The question now, some fifteen years later, is why terrorists or criminals apparently did not take advantage then. One explanation is that they were ignorant, incompetent, and distracted. Another is that the defenses were not as weak as they appeared.

In any case the U.S. government reacted rapidly to a perception of chaos and opportunity in post-Soviet nuclear affairs and in 1993 launched an ambitious complex of "cooperative" programs with all the former Soviet states to lessen the chance that nuclear weapons might end up in the wrong hands. The programs have blossomed into the largest part of American aid to Russia, amounting so far to several billion dollars. There is the undeniable whiff of a protection racket here—of U.S. taxpayers paying off the Russians to please not frighten them—but by the profligate standards of government spending, the money has been well used.

There have been two main efforts. The first, managed by the U.S. Department of Defense, has concentrated on getting Russia to consolidate, secure, and to some degree destroy nuclear warheads, as well as some of the missiles, aircraft, and submarines that carry them. The same cooperative programs have facilitated the spectacular denuclearization of the former Soviet Union's outlying nations. Of particular note is Kazakhstan, which was assisted in abandoning its entire force of 1,400 strategic warheads and 104 intercontinental ballistic missiles—an arsenal that would have made it the world's third largest nuclear-weapons power. The denuclearization of Kazakhstan alone was an important victory for the governments of Russia and the United States, and there have been others, similar in kind.

But these were the maneuverings of conventional actors following the familiar logic of strike and counterstrike. By comparison the perceived vulnerability of nuclear fuel in the former Soviet Union has presented the United States with a wilderness of unknowns. Securing these stocks is the second main cooperative effort. The job has been given primarily to the U.S. Department of Energy, and specifically to officials there with experience managing the American nuclear-weapons infrastructure—a group now formed into a semiautonomous agency known as the National Nuclear Security Administration, or NNSA.

The NNSA sends managers from Washington and technicians from the U.S. national laboratories to supervise foreign officials and oversee the expenditure of American funds. The budget is large: for nonproliferation in 2007 alone, the NNSA has been allocated $1.7 billion. Roughly half of that goes to American over-

head and administrative expenses, but the rest is spent directly
on tightening nuclear safeguards in the former Soviet states. The
work involves cleaning out the smallest and most vulnerable
HEU and plutonium storage sites, improving the physical and
operational security of the larger sites, improving the security of
truck and rail transportation, strengthening the nuclear regulations, and computerizing the material accounting systems to
make losses stand out quickly when they occur. Peripherally,
it also involves shutting down a few reactors, disposing of some
fissile material, and valiantly trying to invent alternative occupa-
tions for idled scientists and technicians in the secret cities—an
effort that usually comes down to just giving them "grants."
These tasks have by now almost been completed in the outlying
nations—a success directly related to the abandonment of nuclear weapons. But of course the center of the effort is in Russia,
where for exactly the opposite reason much work remains to be
done.

In Moscow recently a Russian nuclear official complained to
me about how much of the American funding the American bureaucracy itself consumes. He said, "They send so many people
because they presume that we may deceive them. And we don't
mind. But it is too bad that out of this aid more than half is left in
the United States. This makes us nervous. This is unpleasant." I
answered that Washington's inefficiency should perhaps not be
his worry, and that less than half of $1.7 billion annually still
seems like a lot of money to me. He chuckled, but because of the
size of Russia's nuclear stockpiles, he did not agree.

The frontline agents of the NNSA would take his side. They
tend to be hands-on technical people, impatient to pour concrete
and get the jobs done. Their impulses lie primarily in an area
known as Material Protection Control and Accounting, or within

the NNSA, lovingly, as MPC&A. In brief, this means locking the fissile materials down. Over the years the NNSA has identified 220 buildings at fifty-two sites in Russia that are in dire need of treatment. That's a lot, and as a result, there are actually two treatments. This first is a stopgap measure called a rapid upgrade. It involves bricking up the windows of warehouses, installing stronger locks, fixing the fences, maybe hiring some guards. The second is a long-term fix, called a comprehensive upgrade. It involves the full range of Americanized defenses, including crash-resistant fences, bombproof buildings, remote cameras and electronic sensors, bar-coded inventory scanners, advanced locks, well-armed, well-motivated guards, and all sorts of double- and triple-safe procedures.

Such complex constructs require constant care. Agents of the NNSA see evidence already that the Russians are not committed to maintenance and operations, and some have complained privately to me that as soon as the U.S. funding ends, their elegant MPC&A systems will slip into disrepair. Nonetheless, the NNSA is supposed to wrap up the program, squeeze off the funding, and turn over all the required security upgrades to the Russians, fully completed, within another few years. Knowledgeable observers are skeptical that the schedule can be maintained. They say for instance that a third of the identified buildings have yet to be secured, that these contain about half of Russia's entire fissile material stock, and that they sit at some of the most sensitive sites in the country—areas within the closed cities, where warheads are assembled, and where the NNSA representatives, who have never been welcomed, are increasingly seen as meddlers and spies. The NNSA insists that it will finish the job on budget and on time. Whether such plans are realistic or even desirable, they are what Congress demands, and although no one has said this to me, I suppose that goals can at the last minute be redefined. So there is no reason for anxiety here. One of the beauties of government work is the chance it gives people to stay in their lanes, even as global guerrillas go poking around.

This is not a criticism of the NNSA, but a recognition of its institutional nature. The agency's administrator, a portly former submarine commander and strategic-weapons negotiator named Linton F. Brooks, put it plainly to me when I met him in Washington, D.C. He said, "We are about giving governments the tools to work in those areas where governments have control." Fine. Brooks is an impressive man, and all the more so for his lack of theatrics. He did not pretend to be winning a war, or even to be fighting one, but more simply to be driving up the costs and complications for would-be nuclear bombers. That was his lane, and in these matters he made no grander claims: the NNSA's job is to shift the odds and increase the likelihood that its opponents will fail. It cannot dictate to the Russians. It cannot operate with anything like the flexibility of the terrorists. But of all the U.S. agencies recently engaged to suppress the nuclear threat, it does seem one of the few that may have contributed something real, even if it has to be called MPC&A.

By contrast the CIA seems to have added little to the effort. Presumably its people tag along on some of the technical missions, but they seem largely just to pursue conventional governmental information—estimating military capacities, or mapping the Russian bureaucracy in order to predict Russian reactions. I spoke to a former high U.S. official who said that during a decade spent securing stockpiles in Russia and receiving countless intelligence briefings, he had never once found useful information of the sort that would have helped him to calibrate the risks specific to a site. Who lives in the neighborhood? Who lives just outside?

Who has perhaps just arrived? How the hell do any of them survive? What is meant here, tangibly, by organized crime? Who drives the flashy cars? What are the emotions of the people who do not? How much is known in the street about shipments to and from and between the plants? How much is known about what goes on inside? What do people think about new walls and fences? What do they feel when they see an American flag? Now start all over again, and tell us about the nuclear technicians, the FSB agents, and the ordinary guards. Tell us about their lovers, their holidays, the furniture they dream of buying at IKEA. Tell us about their inner lives.

The official sighed with resignation. I suppose he felt what many believe, that if the United States is hit someday with an atomic bomb, it will in part be because of Washington's discomfort with informal realms—because of a blindness to the street, amply demonstrated in recent times, which will have allowed some bomb-builder the maneuvering room necessary to get the job done.

If you wanted a bomb, you would need this very thing the U.S. government seems to have lost—a sense for streets that are foreign to you, but can quietly be navigated. I flew to Ekaterinburg, Russia, a city on the Siberian side of the southern Urals, two time zones east of Moscow, in a region of forests and factories. Ekaterinburg is where the tsar and his family were liquidated, where the American U-2 pilot Gary Powers was shot down, and where Boris Yeltsin got his start. It has a single-line metro, a small downtown, and a few hotels. Within a few hours' drive a visitor who is sufficiently discreet can arrive at the perimeter walls and fences of five of Russia's ten closed nuclear cities. They are primarily production sites, and they contain all manner of nuclear goods including warheads in various states of assembly, and several hundred tons of excellent fissile material, much of which is of pure weapons grade. Those materials have never just been lying around; inside the nuclear cities they have been kept at the very least under lock and key. So sensitive are the nuclear cities and other defense sites in the vicinity that the entire region, including Ekaterinburg, was closed to outsiders in Soviet times. Since the Soviet Union was itself largely closed and compartmentalized, the nuclear cities stood within concentric layers of defenses like fortresses within fortresses, like nested Russian dolls. Still more pervasive defenses existed in the residents' minds. Good citizens were expected to inform on their neighbors, as they themselves expected to be informed on, and to rely on all the nested gulags to keep everyone in line.

Describing those years in heavily accented English, one of the Russian plant managers said to me, "All nuclear material was secret. *State* secret! Anyone stealing nuclear material in Soviet Union was committing state crime. He became state criminal! Someone acting against the state! So there was fear. Real fear. People were frightened who worked in the nuclear sphere. If something got lost somewhere—maybe a piece of paper, or materials, or there was a mismatch in the plutonium—a person understood that he would be exiled forever." Hesitating over the right words, the manager said, "But then when this . . . *change* took place, of course the people felt more . . . *freedom*, I would say."

Or a different sort of fear. Even today, with the post-Soviet chaos behind them, residents of the nuclear cities believe that their perimeter walls serve best to keep the riff-raff of Ekaterinburg at bay. But that was not what the plant manager meant to say. He was using the word *freedom* for the American ear, and making a familiar argument for the extension of foreign aid. Speaking of the improvements still necessary at his facility, he continued, "It is a very slow process to integrate this new culture into our society, to switch from fear to comprehension. You can say simply that physical protection in Russia used to be based on human factors, and less on technical devices. And in the United States it was vice versa." He thought about this. He said, *"Da."* He said, "But with freedom in Russia the arrangement has had to change."

The Americans have vigorously agreed. The closed cities and nuclear facilities around Ekaterinburg have received a large portion of the U.S. dollars spent on Russian security upgrades, yet they are the subject of continued wariness by the NNSA and are of still greater concern to independent critics in the United States, who insist that they remain acutely vulnerable to terrorists' thefts. Take for example the closed city of Ozersk, a community of eighty-five thousand people whose existence was so hushed under the Soviets that the location was not allowed a proper name and was referred to only by its post office box numbers—first #40, then #65—in Chelyabinsk, an open city forty-four miles away. The nomenclature remains confused. Ozersk is often and mistakenly called Mayak, for its nuclear-production area—an industrial district by that name that stands within the city's outer perimeter, a few miles from the residential center. The Mayak Production Association currently employs 14,500 people, and since 1945 has primarily been in the business of processing HEU, plutonium, and tritium for nuclear warheads. Recently it has also thrown the business into reverse, as one of two sites in Russia where fissile material from existing warheads is extracted before shipment to another closed city for blending down. Many tons of the highest-quality weapons-grade HEU and plutonium are present at the site.

And *nyet*, this is not a state secret.

Divulging it is not a state crime.

Start with the all-American fact that Mayak is the location of the recently completed "Plutonium Palace," a heavily fortified $350 million warehouse, which was paid for by the U.S. Congress and has therefore been heavily publicized. The facility was designed to hold as much as 40 percent of the Russian military's excess fissile material. For now the storage vaults remain empty because of technical and bureaucratic disputes, as well as a sense, in a Russia on the rise, of not wanting to place nuclear assets quite so far out of reach just yet. Nonetheless, there is little doubt that such a beautiful facility will eventually be used—and that the world will be better off when it is.

For those trying to counter the threat of nuclear terrorism, however, the possibility exists that the Palace is just another Maginot fort, a strongpoint that can neatly be ignored by the new strategists of war. The reason, quite simply, is that the Palace will neither reduce nor protect the large quantities of weapons-grade materials elsewhere in Ozersk. NNSA technicians have struggled to fill the gaps, installing cameras and radiation monitors, and strengthening some floors and walls—but only on a few buildings of the many where they believe such work is needed, and only intermittently, under strict guard, as the Russians have allowed. The Russians have made it clear that they are concerned less about thieves or terrorists than about American spies.

By perverse logic, therefore, Ozersk comes highly recommended to anyone in pursuit of a bomb. The combined facilities stand tucked away two hours south of Ekaterinburg, some distance down unmarked back roads, on a forested plateau of lakes and small rivers that would seem idyllic were it not for a number of decimated industrial towns and villages, one with a grim prison, others with moribund factories and sooty apartment blocks in severe disrepair. Outside of Ozersk, it seems that there is not much work left to do—maybe some woodcutting, truck driving, or tinkering with cars. Maybe some summer farming. People walk beside the roads and stop to watch when cars pass by. They linger outside small markets, in doorways, and on forest tracks. They look stolid, stoic, sometimes drunk, and generally wary. Despite their misery, however, these are the sorts of Russians who keep delivering their sons to the Russian conscript army, at a time when the elites are ducking away. They are provincials without privilege, harboring resentments as provincials do, but also, ultimately, forming the backbone of the country; they are the reason, historically, why Russia has been able to fend off all invaders. A bomb-maker would have to possess at least that much sense for the street. The people who inhabit Ozersk's approaches may not run straight to the FSB, but they will remember a stranger and cannot safely be enlisted in a plan to acquire nuclear materials.

Adding to the complexity of the approaches is that this is one of the most contaminated places on earth. That's saying a lot, since particularly in Russia there is such strong competition. The source of contamination is the Mayak production site, which since the start-up of the first reactor in 1948 has been dumping, spilling, bleeding, burning, and raining radioactive waste into the surrounding forests, waters, and towns. For a hundred miles downstream on the banks of a poisoned river called the Tetcha, residents have been forced from the land. There and elsewhere in the vicinity, tens of thousands of people have suffered such unusual exposure that Soviet doctors were able to diagnose a med-

ical condition said to be a first—a disease now called chronic radiation sickness. The initial symptoms include fatigue, weakness,
sleeplessness, headaches, dizziness, nausea, reduced memory,
and pain. For reasons of state security, doctors were forbidden to
explain to their patients what ailed them, or to make reference to
radiation in the medical records; instead the sickness was to be
called the Astheno-Vegetative Syndrome, or more simply the
Special Disease. People figured out the basics, but had to wait
until after the collapse of the Soviet system for files to be declassified, and details to emerge. In the mid-1990s the Norwegian
government funded a comprehensive assessment, largely out of
concern that dangerous quantities of the radioactive waste currently stored at Ozersk will drift northward through the river system and into the Arctic Ocean. In 1997 the study concluded that
the contamination is worse even than imagined, that the Mayak
facilities have spewed at least twice as much dangerous radiation
into the environment as have Chernobyl and all the world's at-
mospheric bomb tests combined, and that underground lobes of
radiation are currently migrating from Mayak's waste-storage
reservoirs.

International environmentalist groups have reacted noisily,
sending fact finders to dig up local cancer cases and examples of
tragic genetic mutations, and mounting some publicity cam-
paigns. But cleaning up the mess there would be unimaginably
expensive, and perhaps impossible. Furthermore, though Russia
is no longer the Soviet Union, it shows little tendency toward
perestroika at its nuclear-weapons sites—and absolutely no patience there with missionaries and crusaders. This has been difficult for some people to accept. In 2004, for example, a group of
Russian environmentalists and sociologists calling themselves
Planet of Hopes requested permission to conduct an opinion sur-

vey inside Ozersk on the subject of ecological and social problems, the transparency of city government, and any known "human rights" abuses. The authorities were not amused. They denied the request, then charged the principal researcher with espionage. The charge was soon dropped, but one of the government's captive newspapers, the mass-circulation *Komsomolskaya Pravda*, subsequently published an article repeating the accusations, and asserting that the group had received money from its "friends in the CIA." The activists were outraged, of course, and they threatened to sue. But it turned out that their work had indeed been financed by a murky American group—not the CIA, but a publicly funded Reagan-era holdover called the National Endowment for Democracy, which agitates for American agendas abroad and seems likely to have U.S. intelligence ties.

Which begs the question of what anyone thought could be learned from the opinion survey in Ozersk, or why the Russian government even bothered with such a minor definition of spies. Elements of simple reactionary spite were perhaps involved, but the attack against Planet of Hopes seems to have had little to do with embarrassment or fear, or with protecting nuclear secrets. Rather it was a public parable, in which an activist "nongovernmental" group stands for the arrogance of intrusive foreigners, and the accusation of spying is understood as a reassertion of Russian pride. Among ordinary Russians, including the residents of the contaminated towns surrounding Ozersk, the story goes down well. This is what a visiting bomb-maker would need to know. It is paradoxical but apparently true that the same people who have suffered from their proximity to a nuclear-production site, and who are angry for having been inadequately compensated, are nonetheless willing to set their problems aside to turn against agitators who come to their region because of the mishandling of radioactive waste. Their willingness encourages local officials, and particularly the agents of the FSB, and this in turn is why the local contamination becomes relevant even to a visitor unconcerned about the environment. Already in Washington, I was warned that for my own safety it would be important to avoid suspicion especially that I might be traveling for Greenpeace.

The conclusion for anyone hunting a bomb's worth of HEU is that few opportunities exist where you might expect to find them, in the communities surrounding the site, and that it is necessary to proceed to Ozersk itself with the utmost discretion. Ozersk's perimeter is large. It encloses more than fifty square miles and includes the city itself, the Mayak production facilities, a network of paved and dirt roads, an internal bus service, one large internal checkpoint (on a divided road, approaching Mayak), multiple railroad lines, burial sites for radioactive waste, multiple radioactive lakes, a lot of radioactive forest, and some radioactive swamps. The main gate is on the north side. It has pens where Interior Ministry troops check vehicles going in or out and verify people's papers. The perimeter is marked by twin parallel chain-link, barbed-wire fences, separated by a chemically defoliated strip that is apparently not mined or raked or checked for tracks even in the snow. The fences are in reasonable repair, but they have no road beside them and show no signs of being patrolled. If they are monitored remotely, it is safe to assume that they are not monitored well. On the south side of the site, they run through miles of empty forest. They could be crossed almost anywhere with little notice, though the chance would be high of eventually being caught, and the consequences would be severe.

And to what advantage? Even if you could get in through the gate, you wouldn't learn much of practical importance by simply walking the streets. You might be able to send in agents who could establish residency, but that would require too much time and offer a poor chance of success. Better to back off and think things through, particularly since the essentials of life there can be known from the outside:

The inhabitants of Ozersk, having suffered discouragement in the 1990s, are feeling a little more hopeful now and tend to think of themselves, still, as among the elites. They are generally well educated, and most are well-enough paid to afford a family car, a restaurant meal every few weeks, and a modest annual holiday trip. On weekends some slip away to Chelyabinsk taverns for evenings of freedom and fun; some go higher into the Urals, depending on the season, to pick mushrooms and berries, or to ski. Otherwise there is little reason locally to leave home. The fashion currently is to open up the gloomy Khrushchev-era apartments by knocking out interior walls, and building American-style countertops to separate the living rooms from the kitchens. People's taste in furnishings is bright, light, and modern. Their entire residential district is tidy and pleasant compared to those of the neighboring towns. It is built between three lakes and has narrow beaches along several shores, where during the few weeks of each short summer the city's inhabitants can collectively turn their skins from white to red or brown. Swimming is probably not a good idea, although these lakes are upslope from those next door at Mayak, and therefore perhaps no more radioactive than the city itself. So pick your poison, but the city does offer choices, and beyond even the standard domestic ones. It has a theater with a puppet stage, four palaces of culture, two libraries with a million books combined, two cinemas, several gymnasiums and playing fields, many clubs, one children's eco-center, and for those quiet afternoons of self-improvement, a municipal museum. It also has no fewer than twenty-three primary and secondary schools (two of which offer extensive studies in English), two sports schools, two music schools, one polytechnical college, one technical university (distinction unclear), and branches of both the Chelyabinsk and Ekaterinburg universities.

Private enterprise is encouraged, but according to one local newspaper, "The Federal State Unitary Enterprise, 'Production Association Mayak,' still takes the leading place in the industrial potential of the town." To say the least. Though 9 percent of registered workers are employed by small enterprises (mostly shops and services), and others work for the city government and in the schools, more than 90 percent of Ozersk's industry is occupied with what is euphemistically referred to as the chemical, machine-building, and metalworking sectors. There are attempts to diversify. The South Urals Vodka Distillery, for instance. And a manufacturer named Bur-Invest, which talked the British government into underwriting the production of what it describes as "ecologically safe wooden furniture for preschool children." And a group of former weapons designers who bravely call themselves Ozersk Confectionery and intend to sell their sugar-cream, flaky puff pastries throughout the Urals and Siberia.

In other words, Ozersk is in the nuclear business and nothing else. Its weapons-usable HEU is kept in Mayak as oxidized powder, flat metal pucks, elongated ingots, and finely machined warhead hemispheres. Each of the HEU forms is stored in a different type of steel container. The containers are light because their shielding is minimal. They are sealed but not locked. They sit on racks in vaults or ordinary storage rooms in eighteen buildings, or sometimes twenty. In addition to the standard containers, larger, brightly colored shipping containers are used to transport the material to and from other nuclear cities and sites. The shipping is done by truck and rail. The shipments are guarded lightly or not at all. In Mayak the empty shipping containers are sometimes kept outdoors. High-resolution satellite photographs available on the Internet show them stacked in the yards, and in other ways help to identify the buildings that count. It does not matter that the photographs are old. Any of thousands of ordinary workers at Mayak could update them and also provide information on material-processing schedules, NNSA upgrades, broken cameras, the patterns of the night shifts, and the locations of guards who use narcotics or drink on the job. It would not be difficult to find such an informant—for instance in the taverns of Chelyabinsk—though of course the arrangement would be dangerous for everyone involved. Afterward the action would have to be fast and accurate. Moving through the forest from the east or south perimeter fences, a raiding party on foot could hit any of the buildings within two hours. This would hardly be a sure thing, because Mayak has defenses all of its own, backed by armed guards, and then there would be the whole huge problem of the getaway. Ten years ago would have been a better time to try. But with luck it could still be done.

Or so knowledgeable Americans urgently believe. Some of the best of them work for a richly endowed organization known as the Nuclear Threat Initiative (NTI), which was founded by former senator Sam Nunn and the CNN mogul Ted Turner in 2001 to advocate for various forms of nuclear disarmament. The director of NTI's efforts in the former Soviet Union is a smart, no-nonsense Washington insider named Laura Holgate, who spent years as a senior U.S. official grappling with Russian nuclear-weapons security. When we met at NTI's strangely buttoned-up Washington headquarters, she repeated a colleague's anecdote about a certain closed city where informal parking lots have sprung up outside holes in the fence, because workers prefer not to bother with the gate.

But I wanted to know about Ozersk, which seems to be more orderly, perhaps because of the quantities of bomb materials there. She had visited it as a member of an official delegation. I asked about the security upgrades. She answered indirectly, "It's a very challenging environment to work in. You set up a radiation detector, and it's constantly on. Or someone transplants a tree, and *it* sets off the detector. So how are you supposed to catch the illicit movement of material as unradioactive as HEU? There's so much clandestine movement of everything—cooking oil, insulation, you name it. They put a little box of uranium in the corner, and they're fine." Moreover, the Russian government, she implied, can be somewhat dismissive about such matters.

Later, in Russia, I spoke to a modest American technician with a decade of experience in the secret cities of the Urals. He knew enough of Washington to want to remain anonymous, but did not seem interested in diplomatic maneuvering or nuclear policy. He was a detail man, a practitioner. He said, "Some of what the NNSA puts in is worthwhile, maybe. And other stuff seems, ah, not to get used. I took a tour one time, and they had installed a radiation monitor, a portal, for traffic going in and out of the site. So I say, 'So, how's the portal working?'

"And this Russian says, 'Oh, we shut it off most of the time.'

" 'Why?'

" 'Because it's always going off.'

" 'How come it always goes off?'

"He says, 'Well . . . it's the people on the buses. People go fishing in the lake, and when they catch fish and bring them out on the bus, they set off the radiation monitor. And then we've got to respond.' "

The technician laughed at his own story. Just when you think you've nabbed a terrorist, what you've really nabbed is a radioactive fish. After ten years around Russia's nuclear facilities, he was not concerned. He said, "But you know, things like radiation portals? That's just *our* method of security. They've got their own methods, which are probably as effective."

"You mean human intelligence?"

"Yeah. It's more *people* intensive, the way they do it."

I told him about my conversation with the Russian plant manager who had argued for the need to change to American ways, and I mentioned my suspicion that however amiably the Russian was playing me for a fool. As I remembered the conversation, I had finished by asking the plant manager why a country as competent as Russia would even bother with American advice on its own nuclear security.

The technician said, "It must have been funny what he answered."

"He was sort of shifty. But basically he said, 'So long as Americans are willing to give us money, we'll be willing to take it.' "

The technician said, "Yeah, I think basically that's it."

The terrain is difficult to assess. Others have described Ozersk's human side in the sort of dire terms that would give you hope if you were trying to build a bomb—children selling narcotics in the schools, mobsters in the construction and trucking businesses, and large numbers of unvetted Central Asians arriving to do menial work that would before have been reserved for loyal Slavs. The worst of the lot are said to be the soldiers whose duty is to guard the site. Called "the dregs of the dregs" by some critics, they are second-round conscripts, picked up by the Interior Ministry only after they have been rejected by the Russian army. They in no sense constitute an elite corps, as the ministry sometimes claims. NTI has catalogued a string of known incidents in which Mayak's guards killed each other, committed suicide, stole weapons, ran away, bought narcotics, drank on duty, and in one case imbibed a bottle of antifreeze and died.

As to what American experts believe such a raid might look like, there is no need to wonder: in 2005, NTI produced a "docudrama" about nuclear terrorism, entitled *Last Best Chance*, which was shown on HBO television and is now distributed freely to almost anyone who asks. Holgate mentioned that a copy was requested by a certain Ousama Bin Laden, in Brussels, and that no copy was sent—but that's how far you have to go not to get it. The DVD arrives in a colorful cardboard envelope, which claims on the back that the film is based on fact, though more honestly it is based on possibility. The film portrays Washington officials in embarrassingly self-important roles, but otherwise is less insulting to viewers than might be expected. It depicts a hostile raid of the sort that NTI and its assembled experts earnestly believe could occur at facilities like those of Mayak. Black-clothed mercenaries break into a nuclear warehouse at night, extract some HEU from a sealed container, replace it with material of equal weight, reseal the container, then kill a hapless guard and their own guide and make off with a bomb's worth of fuel into the wilds of a post-Soviet night. Care was taken with the technical details. The action is superficially convincing. The actors portraying the mercenaries are impressively taut. They possess Germanic qualities of speed, efficiency, and orientation, which second-round Russian conscripts evidently do not.

The problem for you, in your quest for a bomb, is that in the real world even second-round conscripts will fight. This is less a possibility than a fact. They will fight whether sober or drunk. Their presence at Ozersk means that no raiding party, even of picture-perfect warriors, will be able to hit any of the storage buildings without provoking a noisy response. American specialists have warned that a large and coordinated attack could nonetheless overwhelm or counter traditional Russian defenses, and they have pointed to the Chechen seizure of a Moscow theater in 2002, and the similar seizure of a Beslan school two years later, as evidence that terrorists within Russia already possess the wherewithal. Often cited is a Russian newspaper story that the theater raiders had first explored the idea of attacking a Moscow nuclear-research campus called the Kurchatov Institute, where several tons of HEU are kept. Whether true or not, for the Americans this is good news disguised as bad. The Kurchatov Institute has benefited more than any other nuclear site in Russia from collaboration with the United States, and it has put in place a large number of American-style security upgrades. It has become popular to suggest that the upgrades might have impressed the Chechens and frightened them away. Omitted from the scenario, however, is the question of whether the raiders knew about fissile material, or what they could have done with it once they were surrounded by thousands of Russian troops and were themselves being secured by traditional Russian means.

Authorities in Ozersk reacted to the Moscow attack by tightening the defenses not of the fissile materials at Mayak, but of the residential district between the lakes—a move equivalent to keeping the dreaded Ekaterinburgers at bay. Why would any group of raiders choose a Russian closed city as a location to take hostages and die a public death? The sole purpose of an attack on Ozersk would be nearly the opposite—to obtain weapons-grade

HEU as quickly and quietly as possible, then escape with it beyond the horizons to some secret place where a bomb could be assembled. You can imagine alternatives—for instance stashing the material nearby or even inside the perimeter for a while— but the risk in every case would be of having been too clever by far. Better to run hard for an international boundary and leave Russia behind.

The getaway factor is not often raised in the United States, where the focus on Russian nuclear facilities and store-bought solutions allows a view to prevail of a Wild West environment in which a nuclear bandit would need only to ride out of town in order to vanish safely. It is not by chance that in *Last Best Chance* the van carrying stolen HEU disappears by simply driving away from the camera. But up close to Ozersk and thinking practically, if you wanted to mount a raid, you would keep running across evidence of a powerful and self-confident Russia that seems to be more like its old autocratic self, and at least selectively under control.

When I mentioned my impression to a Russian nuclear expert who has been the recipient of American grants, he strongly agreed and, to my surprise, attacked the hand that has been feeding him. He was particularly irritated by an influential group of Harvard specialists who track the minutiae of nuclear diplomacy and the cooperative programs and have done some necessary work, but may with time and repetition have ossified. Speaking of them, the Russian said, "These people who express such concerns about Russia in the United States. I know them well, and they are my friends, but they are like mammoths trapped in a freeze. They make money from this and have for twenty years. I do not mind. But they're lagging far behind. Their brains have not advanced. Even when they come here, their thoughts are far away."

A more generous view is that professional observers in the United States have had little reason not to widen their worries, even in their private thoughts, and that this expansion has allowed them to play a useful public role—though one requiring the audience to understand the forces affecting their careers. The demise of the Soviet Union and subsidence of the Cold War dangers might have nudged them into obscurity, had it not been for the related rise of a terrorist nuclear threat. As it happened, they were able to sidestep elegantly into the new area of concern in the 1990s, and then, following the terrorist attacks of 2001, to prosper. The knowledge they brought to the subject was real. Russia did have loose nukes and still today presents the best opportunities for anyone trying to acquire fissile material. But the American experts have been working in a murky and dangerous area, where a declaration of safety can at any time be proved spectacularly wrong, and they may indeed therefore have littered the scene with obsolete or irrelevant concerns.

By contrast, as a bomb-maker you would not widen your worries, but narrow them down. The nearest international border to Ozersk is with Kazakhstan, only four hours' drive to the south, but the route is poor, because it runs through the city of Chelyabinsk and crosses border checkpoints using roads that on either side of the line can easily be blocked. Furthermore Kazakhstan is a developed authoritarian state, with strong police controls, that has divested itself of nuclear arms and is clearly not the right place for nuclear fugitives to hide. A safer plan would be to remain inside Russia and head southwest, twelve hundred miles or more, for the Caspian Sea or the Caucasus, with the goal of crossing the uranium to Turkey through Azerbaijan, Armenia, Georgia, or northern Iran. The trip would, however, require at least three days just for the escape from Russia—an interval that becomes the minimum head start required, if any plan is to succeed, before the loss of material is even noticed at Mayak. And raiders would be lucky to have three hours. In good conscience therefore (if perhaps with some relief), a rational bomb-maker would abandon any idea of commando heroics.

But that is not to say you would give up on Ozersk. Possibilities abound for an insider job, and though the deal would be fraught with the chance of betrayal, the potential advantages are huge: insiders could neutralize any practical defenses, pass through the gates with a load of unshielded HEU undetected, and provide a getaway team with a head start that could be measured in weeks or months—perhaps right up to the time when an assembled bomb ignites. Linton Brooks described the possibility of insider theft as the greatest challenge facing the NNSA in Russia today. The solutions, which can at best only be partial, consist of attempting to complicate the task of would-be thieves, requiring them to bring more people into a conspiracy and to operate with larger teams.

An agent with experience in these matters said, "You try to make it more difficult by putting in doors that require two people to open. You put in video surveillance to make sure there really are two people. You put in watchers to watch the watchers. Finally you put in accounting systems to bring the facilities from paper ledgers into the bar-code era. They had rough inventory practices before, a tendency to keep material off the books to cover for shortfalls in production—stuff hidden away in a garage someplace. Now it's gotten quite a bit better, but there are very deep-seated, long-standing cultural issues here. In the Soviet days you were a very trusted person, an elite person, if you were working in these facilities. And now we come along, and we say, 'Okay, you're not allowed to go into the vault by yourself anymore. You need one or two other people with you every time you unlock the door.' That can take a while to sink in. Also, there's a different perception of rules and regulations. The rule of law is not looked at the same way. There's more skepticism in Russia. It's a very complicated problem. Bricking up windows is part of the solution, but it's not everything."

And it's not as if the Russians don't already know how to build strong rooms. I mentioned to the American technician in the Urals that even ordinary doors in Russia are heavy. He said, "One of the guys at the plant said to me, 'Jack, I watch American movie last night.' " The technician imitated a Russian accent. " 'And I see something strange. Drug police. They kick in door! In Russia, this not possible!' "

Or maybe in Russia, this is not necessary.

We were drinking German beer in a bar just outside one of the nuclear cities, a place where the technician was not allowed to live, but into which he was escorted every day under guard to do his job. I asked him about the mood inside. He said, "It's amazing the changes. Used to be the grocery store was ninety percent empty shelves, a desolate-looking place, beat-up, birds flying around inside. You had to do the three-line shuffle. You'd go in and go through a line at the potato bin. You'd want a couple of potatoes, and so when you'd get to the potato lady, you'd say, 'Gimme two potatoes.' And she'd write up a sales slip for you. Then you'd go to another line for the cashier, and you'd go through that line, and you'd pay. The cashier would stamp your slip. And then back you'd go to the first line again. You'd go through that whole line again, and when you'd get to the potato lady, she'd give you your two potatoes."

I said, "And now?"

"Now they've got a supermarket every bit as nice as Safeway. And they've got everything in it. Used to be I'd say, 'Boy, you oughta taste these drinks called margaritas, but you need lime to make them. And tequila.' And they'd say, 'What's lime?' You know? And now you can buy lime, avocado, the whole works. Almost anything you can buy in L.A. you can buy here. And the Russians are going through that place like mad. You just can't believe how much they're buying." He nursed his beer. He said, "There seems to be a lot of money in town." He thought it through. He said, "And yet the guys I work with don't make that much."

"So what's the explanation?"

"I'm not sure. That's a mystery."

A culture of wealth without explanation certainly broadens the opportunities for recruiting thieves. As does the related culture of corruption. The technician was aware of the possibility of an inside job. He said, "The guy I'd be worried about is the plant director."

"One guy by name?"

"Naw, just generally."

I said, "But he's probably too high."

"Yeah, you're right. He wouldn't have the access."

"The HEU is kept locked up?"

"There's a two-person system of control."

"And who are these people?"

"They're regular workers. Regular people."

"And if you get to those people and give each of them five

million dollars, could they walk out carrying one hundred pounds of HEU? Are there other security measures?"

"There's almost always another two people there, so you'd have to get to four people."

"Almost always?"

"And then there are usually guards on the outside of the building."

"But mentally they're facing outward, right? Would it be possible for workers to mask an illicit movement as a normal one?"

"They've got a special truck for transportation. Maybe the driver is the guy to buy."

But these were details for later. I got back to the cultural questions. "And what about all the expensive cars I've seen around here?"

"Some people are making money."

"Does anyone mind?"

He said, "There's this area inside the city that has these *big* houses. Big new houses. I mean, huge. Like five thousand square feet. I went into one that was being built. It was beautiful, with a cabana, a recreation room, a swimming pool. Beautiful. And inside the city! The way I got in—I bribed a guard. I'd love to have that house."

He seemed to have Cinco de Mayo parties in mind.

I said, "So what is it, the mob?"

"There's always that joke."

"What joke?"

"The mob. I haven't seen any, but I'm sure they're around."

"How would you identify them?"

"That's the thing. I wouldn't know."

I said, "I guess most would look like businessmen."

"Yeah, that's right."

"But go back to the houses. What's the explanation?"

He said, "I asked my friends about it."

"What did they say?"

"They said it's the plant manager's." He looked doubtful.

I said, "But . . ."

"But these houses are *big*! And there are probably a couple dozen of them. They started popping up in the last two years."

"So nobody knows the real answer?"

"Nobody I know knows. They're all workers. I don't think they ask a lot of questions."

With one hundred pounds of stolen HEU split between a couple of knapsacks, and a healthy head start on Russian security forces, you would not have to worry much about getting caught by Americans. The United States claims to be building a layered defense, but the only layer that amounts to much is the NNSA's securing of stockpiles—and we can suppose that you have just penetrated it with the help of workers at the site. At this point the American and European defenses fall spectacularly apart. The reasons are ultimately institutional and complex, but may initially be as simple as confusion created by the expanding geometry of choices for anyone carrying HEU toward an assembly point for the construction of a bomb. Will you go left or right? The roads keep forking, forcing you to turn one way or the other, often for no more discernible reason other than that forward motion requires a choice. Western officials who would try to stop you face an infinite braid that becomes the measure of a hostile and anarchic world.

In Washington I spoke to one of the many officials in town who, though carrying out their assignments reasonably well, are too nervous about domestic politics to dare being identified. He described an NNSA effort called the Second Line of Defense, which installs radiation monitors at border crossing points throughout the former Soviet Union, and especially along the likely smuggling routes of Central Asia and the Caucasus. South of Russia, the program is most fully developed in the troubled republic of Georgia, a skeletal nation threatened by separatist enclaves and barely able to keep warm through the winters. The official said, "The Corps of Engineers is working with U.S. Customs to build whole new border-crossing facilities in Georgia, and we're in the process of installing upgraded radiation monitors, in conjunction with that."

I said, "I guess I can see the logic of the radiation monitors, but why are we building customs stations for the Georgians?"

"It's a joint venture to try to control smuggling."

It's amazing. Georgia is one of the most corrupt nations on earth. Many of its politicians are crooks. Its officials routinely steal. Its economy is based almost entirely on black markets. Its people have nothing to survive on if they do not hustle. I said, "Why should we care about ordinary smuggling in Georgia? Cigarettes? Vodka? Fuel? For that matter, narcotics?" What I meant was, if even the ordinary black markets of Georgia are seen as a threat, where does the impulse to impose order end?

He stayed in his lane, but executed a tidy reversal: "It's a good question. And I don't know that I have the answer, but the genesis anyway was nuclear. So I guess in conjunction with our new equipment, it makes sense for Customs to upgrade the stations."

This is how government works: in urgent response to the attacks of September 11, the U.S. Customs Service was absorbed into the new U.S. Department of Homeland Security, where it was combined with the U.S. Border Patrol into a new agency named U.S. Customs and Border Protection, or CBP. Officially the CBP says that it is "the executive agent for a Congressionally mandated multi-agency Border Security and Related Law Enforcement Assistance Program to the former Soviet Republic of Georgia."

Hoping to get some sense for the realities, I went to Tbilisi, the capital of Georgia, and the next morning headed over to the magnificent new monumental-bunker-style U.S. embassy on the outskirts of the city, for an interpretation. The Americans there had said they were willing to talk about the program, but now, with their public-relations minder sitting nervously in, they were so guarded that even off the record they ended up saying nothing at all. In any case they seemed to be winding down in anticipation of a three-day federal weekend, I forget which one.

Georgian officials were more forthcoming. When I mentioned my surprise that expensive improvements are being made to the ports of entry while the rest of the border remains utterly uncontrolled, a senior officer of the Georgian Border Guards nodded sympathetically and said there was some history I needed to know. He said the United States had initially given them funds to buy three helicopters from Ukraine, with which to fly patrols. They had acquired two of the helicopters, and although one of them was then grounded for lack of spare parts, the other was still being flown, and by a daredevil Border Guard pilot who gives thrilling rides and is also a great guy. Problems arose, however, over the third helicopter, which appeared to have been paid for, but never showed up in town. Americans do not normally care about wastage, the officer explained. For example they insist on supplying the Border Guards with desktop computers billed to American foreign-aid accounts at more than twice the price for which the same computers can be bought in Tbilisi stores. Nonetheless they were annoyed by the disappearance of an entire helicopter's worth of dollars. He said they reacted by reasserting control over American capital-improvement funds and quietly announcing that henceforth the big money would be spent only on immovable objects that are awkward to sell and impossible to fly away.

Ports of entry fit the bill. I drove south to the model project, a station dubbed Red Bridge by the Americans, which stands at the main crossing point between Georgia and Azerbaijan. The first improvement there was the construction of a housing compound on flat ground, where rotating units of the Border Guards had previously been camping in tents and cooking their meals over open fires. By the time the U.S. Department of Homeland Security was finished with it, in 2003, the compound consisted of five single-family houses, a barracks for sixty-four men, a dining hall, an administration building, a vehicle-maintenance garage, a warehouse for supplies, an armory, various utility buildings, a dog kennel, two water-storage buildings, a sewage plant, an electrical substation, a perimeter fence, two guard towers, two helipads, a sports field, a separate soccer field, some new paved roads and parking lots, and, of course, a parade ground. After the official opening, a U.S. Customs and Border Protection newsletter asked the CBP project manager, James Kelly, "Is it as grand as it sounds?"

"Indeed it is," Kelly said. "It was built to Western standards."

Golly, and that was merely Phase One. The United States then shifted its spending down the road to the port of entry itself, where Georgian customs officials were using shipping containers with holes cut in the sides as offices and booths. Over the following two years, the U.S. government oversaw the construction of a $2.2 million facility, whose primary purpose, according to the

CBP, would be to "help Georgia become a more effective partner in the worldwide effort to control the passage of terrorists and their weapons." This time the improvements included a six-lane roadway, comfortable booths, cargo-inspection areas, closed-circuit remote-control television cameras, lots of computers, a high-frequency long-distance radio communication system, and the crowning glory—a beautiful air-conditioned, two-story, stucco-walled building with spaces for processing the grateful public, as well as detention cells, back offices, a dormitory wing for Georgian customs agents, private sleeping rooms upstairs for American officials and other VIPs, and even a second-floor patio, apparently for sitting outside on warm evenings.

The day I got there was too chilly for that. A short line of trucks crept in from Azerbaijan, and a few cars passed through in the opposite direction, heading south. The new radiation monitors were not yet in place, but within a few weeks they were certain to be. The main building was so empty that it looked as if it were being preserved for some future use as yet unknown. Upstairs, a shiny brass plaque on a locked door read "James F. Kelly Memorial Port of Entry Dining Room, Red Bridge, Georgia, March 2005." My Georgian hosts had never noticed the plaque and had no idea what it was supposed to mean. They were Border Guards from up the road, and this building was a little unfamiliar to them. It was meant to be a shared facility, but was informally understood to be the domain of customs, and the two groups don't get along. When the customs chief heard that I was in the building, he came up and made his rank clear. I asked to see the control room, which is meant to be the nerve center of the operation and would soon contain the meters for the radiation detectors. There was a delay until the key could be found, whereupon the chief showed me in. The room was a windowless refuge, empty except for a few chairs, some computers on a table, and a bank of flat-screen displays. Someone had left a video game on. Someone had left a magazine. Empty cardboard boxes for the equipment stood stacked in a corner. After a while an eager young man came in and demonstrated how a camera on the roof could be swiveled and zoomed.

The anonymous official in Washington tried to explain to me why such improvements matter. I had asked him why anyone carrying HEU would choose to go through any official gate anywhere in the world. He did not predict that anyone would. Using Georgia as an example, he said, "The good news is that there aren't very many of these border crossings. And to the extent we've got them covered, we force people to use horses, I guess."

Horses, mules, donkeys, tractors, dirt bikes, plucky little Ladas—whatever. A bit of off-road travel wouldn't seem like much of an inconvenience to nuclear smugglers on the move, and American officials know it well. The problem is that U.S. agencies, when pressured by conflicting mandates and forced to work with corrupt and dysfunctional local governments, essentially throw up their hands at the complexity of it all and abandon the fight in advance.

To be clear about this, the fight under discussion is not the securing of nuclear stockpiles, nor is it the global war on disorder, but more narrowly, it is the interdiction of any significant load of HEU that has somehow been acquired by a criminal or terrorist group, that is not yet known to have disappeared, and that is illicitly being transported across long distances to an assembly point for an atomic bomb. In that context, Red Bridge is not just a customs post, but a premature surrender—and a typical one. Faced with the need to put systems in place that will function day after day to identify unexpected nuclear smugglers, America turns to the uniformed agents of a corrupt local government, loads them down with air-conditioned buildings and gadgetry, then asks them to sit in a closed room watching for information from television cameras and radiation monitors—to which it paves the roads. To make matters worse, the failure is not individual, but collective, and therefore difficult to correct. It appears to include even the clandestine services, some of which are chasing Al Qaeda around, but none of which shows signs of wanting to lay traplines through the backcountry on the off chance—highly unlikely in any given location—of snaring just two packs' worth of dull gray metal. Of course it is possible that they are doing this, and being so discreet that for once they leave no evidence of their passage, but if you were moving a load of HEU across international borders, you could gamble that they are not.

It is as if the U.S. government, when looking at a world map for the purposes of HEU interdiction, has declared entire regions to be off-limits to anything other than governmental fictions. As might be expected, those regions are where some of the world's principal opium routes lie and, for independent reasons, are the areas through which stolen HEU seems most likely to pass. It is generally assumed that for the right price, opium traffickers will provide transportation, lodging, and expert advice to nuclear terrorists moving through. Indeed the persistence of the drug trade worldwide is often used as an object lesson in the difficulty of trying to stop the smuggling of nuclear materials. A tired joke often repeated is that the best way to transport an atomic bomb is inside a bale of marijuana. The point, of course, is that borders are wide open. The analogy, however, is fundamentally misleading, because a small amout of HEU is worth far more than any conceivable load of narcotics, and it moves in a minuscule marketplace as a one-shot deal, dangerous to everyone involved, difficult to replace, and of infinitely greater importance to stop.

Indeed the proximity between the two trades may seem unfortunate coincidence, but it could be turned into a fortunate one if the differences were exploited in quiet conversation with a few key people. The problem is that those people are not likely to be local officials. Finding them would require casual exploration along the preexisting lines of defense, in remote valleys below high mountain passes, around certain ports, and especially along the national boundaries that cross the smuggling routes—borders aligned primarily east and west in Central Asia, and north and south on the Caucasian side of the Caspian Sea. More fundamental, it would require accepting that regions beyond government control are rarely as chaotic as they seem to be to Western officials. The foundation work for effective interdiction would involve poking around meekly, usually by taxi, sometimes with an amateur translator and guide. The purpose would not be to recruit peasant armies and spies, but to get a feel for the informal or nongovernmental functioning of power. In most areas, only two or three people are at the top, and they tend to be at once aggressive and benevolent men with interests larger than just the movement of drugs. Their names would quickly become apparent. Some might be dangerous to approach, but most would be hospitable to strangers. On the second or third trip back, a Western agent might make it known that if ever a load of genuine HEU showed up, a large bounty would be paid—perhaps in the Red Bridge range. This would require the moralists back home to mute their outrage at deals struck with foreign drug traffickers, but given the stakes it seems they might.

I have a Kurdish friend in Iraq who moves through war with the grace of a dancer. In 2004 at a time of increasing attacks, when Westerners living in Baghdad were urgently hiring Western security companies to install surveillance cameras and elaborately beef up their household defenses, he gave me advice about my own modest quarters, which had a rocket-shattered front end, and a pack of feral dogs living on the street outside. He had advised me before to avoid the fiction of a formal security plan and simply leave the broken glass on the ground and in a stairwell leading down from the roof. Now he added, just feed the dogs.

Some months ago I made the first of two brief trips through the mountains of extreme eastern Turkey, in the Kurdish hinterland along the border with Iran. That border lies across one of the simplest routes to Istanbul from the closed cities of the Urals: through Russia, down the Caspian, and across northwestern Iran. The landscape is immense, with high, snowy peaks, and valleys that span great distances, but the dividing line runs along rounded mountains that can be crossed in about five hours on foot and regularly are. This is the prime smuggling country I mentioned earlier, where every night the pack trains run, bringing in untaxed diesel fuel from Iran, and opium from Afghanistan. The local villages may seem sleepy, but they are wide-awake. After just a few days of wandering around it became apparent to me that the entire region is tightly sewed up, that nothing moves there without notice, and that any transborder activity requires approval. The authority is of course not the Turkish government. The army maintains several checkpoints on the road, which serve not to stop the traffic, but to collect bribes. In one of the villages a young man told me that the army runs patrols at night and sometimes shoots the smugglers' horses.

Maybe. The young man misdirected me away from the smuggling trails, one of which I later followed long enough to verify that it was easily walkable. Primarily the army is here to fight the sporadic guerrilla war against Kurdish separatists, who occasionally ambush a patrol or plant a mine, then retreat higher into the Turkish mountains. The main garrison is in a village called Baskale, which is better known for its heroin labs. When Pakistan was building centrifuges for its nuclear-weapons facilities, some of the more sensitive parts passed through here.

Baskale has a large yellow house in a central compound, which belongs to the leader of a clan that is dominant for miles around, an extended family named Ertosi, which consists of 150,000 to 200,000 people. The house is only sometimes inhabited, when the Ertosi chief wants to show a presence in the community. One afternoon I was invited in for tea. The host was a black-bearded, heavyset middle-aged man who had arrived from Ankara for a few days. He was merely a son of the chief, but was important enough to have guards and flunkies around. We sat against the walls in a large bare room, with photographs of dead Ertosi at one end, and a big-screen television at the other. The television was tuned to a banned Kurdish station, broadcast via satellite from London. My translator introduced me as an English teacher on holiday, which threw our host a little off-balance, I think. He wore a heavy gold chain and a diamond ring. He had an array of cell phones in front of him on the floor, several of which rang. Between the phone calls, I asked him about the diesel trade. He said a little, but clammed up when I got into the practical details. To my translator he said, "Why does an English teacher want to know so much?" We moved on.

Weeks later I returned to the area and sought out a certain sub-clan leader I had heard about. He was a powerful man, the hereditary chief of twenty thousand Ertosi who occupy the most active stretch of the border. He did not have a telephone. I found him in a hamlet perched among patches of snow, high on a mountainside. It was late at night, and the air was cold. We sat among ten of his men in a small stone room around a woodburning stove. He was a small man, sixty years old, with sharp, hooded eyes and a hooked nose. He was dressed like a Kurdish peasant, with a tweed jacket down to his knees. His hands were hardened by manual labor. We avoided mention of narcotics or HEU and talked instead in transparent code about the business in "diesel fuel." He said, "The government cannot control the border. The Kurds just naturally do." We talked about how. The details do not matter right now. No stranger could cross without his knowledge. We talked about women, wives, and life. He told me he has a son who works for an insurance company in Toronto, and a daughter who works as a doctor in the Turkish city of Van. He said that in general he prefers daughters to sons. He wanted me to understand that Kurds treat women right, and to get some feeling for the tradition they have of kidnapping their brides. He described his own administration of justice, and the advantages of traditional Kurdish law. We spoke at length about his clan, of which he was proud. At various points he said, "The other clans are afraid of us because we are brave," and, "The other clans are afraid of us because we live close to nature," and, "The other clans are afraid of us because we have nothing to lose." He said, "You do not need to be afraid of me. You can ask me anything you want." I thanked him for that. Others in the room were nervous about some of my questions, but he was not. As the night passed, he offered to slaughter a sheep in my honor. I sensed that we got along well enough, and that on a second visit I could have broached the subject of uranium—whether as a messenger from the United States, or from its foes.

Assuming you paid attention to leaders like these—and that Western governments continue to ignore them—you would probably succeed in moving the HEU across the borders and finally emerge into the noise and commotion of a country like Turkey, where you could disappear for a while. Then comes the problem of assembly. In choosing a site, you could be certain that no country would dare to be associated with the construction of an independent atomic bomb. Not Libya, not Sudan, not Iran. The certainty of retribution after its use far outweighs whatever benefit might be gained. Moreover you could never trust those governments not to wait until the end and confiscate the goods. So the work would have to be carried out in secret—and in some private machine shop perhaps no larger than a five-car garage. The shop would contain numerically controlled milling machines and lathes, as well as other expensive manufacturing equipment, and would require a plausible explanation—a front company set up to manufacture, say, industrial pumps or automotive transmission components. The best location would seem to be in some freewheeling global city where governmental control is lax, corruption is rampant, and the noise emanating from the shop will be masked by other industrial activities nearby. Take your pick: Mombasa, Karachi, Mumbai, Jakarta, Mexico City, São Paulo, and a short list of others. There are risks and advantages to each of them. Here we might choose Istanbul if for no better reason than to break from the narrative of travel.

Construction of the bomb would take maybe four months.

The size of the technical team would depend on the form of HEU. At the minimum it would consist of a nuclear physicist or engineer, a couple of skilled machinists, preferably with experience in shaping uranium, an explosives expert who can design and handle the propellant, and perhaps an electronics person for the trigger. The essentials of the work are easy to grasp. To repeat the physics: the nuclear chain reaction starts when a single speeding neutron causes a uranium atom to split, or fission, which produces two more neutrons, which find two more atoms to split, and so forth. An ultrafast atom-splitting progression of two, four, eight, sixteen, thirty-two, sixty-four, one hundred twenty-eight, and onward will amount to an explosion, but only if there are sufficient atoms available to keep the reaction going for multiple generations before the neutrons arrive at the surface of the uranium and wastefully fly away through the air. Therefore the critical measure, at any given level of enrichment, for any given shape, is the mass of the metal involved. A cannon-style bomb takes two lumps of HEU, each barely subcritical, and slams them together into one amply critical mass.

But there is a bit more to it than that. As compared to plutonium, and measured against the necessary time scale (an entire generation every ten-millionth of a second), HEU rarely shoots off the first neutron spontaneously. If it *never* did, there would be no trick at all to making a bomb. A weapons designer once told me, "You could have the kids help. Just pile the HEU up. Then when you're good and ready, you fire the first neutron, and, bloop, the pile blows up." But the same characteristics that complicate the transport of HEU, requiring two packs instead of one, also complicate the construction of a bomb: HEU does not sit entirely idle, and every once in a while (in atomic time) it fires off a neutron spontaneously. The main problem that has to be overcome in making a bomb is to join two masses together quickly enough, into a critical whole, before such a random firing occurs.

It's a question partly of luck. Consider that an effective atomic bomb could be made out of nothing more than a stepladder and two seventy-five-pound bricks of 90 percent HEU. You drive to the center of the city that you intend to hit. You place one brick on the sidewalk, climb the ladder with the other brick under your arm, hold it directly overhead, and let it fall. From then on it's a gamble. You win if the two bricks have time to touch before the explosion occurs. You lose if a stray neutron fires early and kicks off the chain reaction before the bricks have time to get close. In military terms this would be called a fizzle, because the chain reaction would barely begin to exploit the combining mass before heat would drive the bricks apart. Fizzle, however, is a relative term. It has been calculated that this one would produce an explosion in the two-kiloton range, which would be enough to level a city block. By contrast, if the neutron fires an instant later, at the optimal moment, the resulting blast could amount to ten kilotons, roughly two-thirds of the way toward a Hiroshima-sized explosion.

A cannon-type bomb can be nearly as simple a device, since its purpose is largely just to improve on the odds of the ladder-bomb design. Instead of bricks, it employs two HEU hemispheres, which when joined together form a single sphere. A sphere is the geometric shape that provides the smallest surface area in relation to mass, lowering the threshold of criticality by allowing fewer neutrons to escape once the nuclear reaction starts. To further limit escape, one of the hemispheres, the receiver, is fixed into a dense metal, typically lead, which reflects some of the fugitive neutrons back into the mass and also delays the explosive expansion, however briefly, thereby allowing more atoms to be split, before the process self-destructs. The receiving hemisphere is hollowed or concave on one side. The other hemisphere, sometimes known as the bullet or the plug, has a perfectly matched convex surface on the opposing side. It sits in wait at the top of a smooth steel barrel about as long as a stepladder is high. When the time comes to detonate the bomb, the plug is shot down the barrel by a measured charge of chemical propellant, which burns progressively to avoid blasting the barrel apart. The ideal velocity for the plug is one thousand yards per second, roughly three times the speed of sound, or about as fast as a fast rifle round. The goal is to slam the masses together before the nuclear reaction has a chance to start prematurely. Once the masses have joined, the HEU can be trusted to do its job, though with such a primitive garage-made device there will be significant differences in the explosive yield, due primarily to variations in the timing and propagation of the chain reaction. Conventional military designs use neutron generators and go to great lengths to deliver predictable yields, while also miniaturizing and securing the bombs. As a result, the warheads built even by such primitive countries as Pakistan tend to be complex. A common misperception about terrorist bombs is that they would mimic such military devices and would therefore require a level of expertise found only in government laboratories. But if you were a terrorist, you would not much care whether you struck, say, New York with a ten- or twenty-kiloton blast, and for secrecy's sake you would strive to keep the design elaborations to a minimum.

Even so, the construction of a bomb is not a casual project. The required machinery, the noise, and especially the presence of team members who are unlikely to be locals provides the West with the last practical chance of self-defense. Your team of bomb-builders would have to keep this clearly in mind. A city like Istanbul, which appears from a distance to be anarchic and is famously resistant to central authority, is in practice a patchwork of tightly knit communities with something of the organic power structures of the borderlands. In even the most chaotic neighborhoods, where industrial shops are mixed among illegal apartment blocks and communities of impoverished newcomers and squatters, it would be difficult to keep the neighbors from asking inconvenient questions. The same is true in Mombasa, Karachi, and every other city where a bomb could conceivably be built: these are urban collectives, ungovernable perhaps, but not necessarily uncontrolled. Western agencies that could find a way to lay traplines in their slums would have a better chance of stopping a terrorist attack than any port-inspection program, bureaucratic reshuffling, or military maneuvering can provide. Here again, though, there is little evidence that Western agencies are capable of emerging from their rigidly governmental frameworks.

In the final analysis, if a would-be nuclear terrorist calculated the odds, he would have to admit that they are stacked against him, simply because of all the natural circumstances that could cause his plans to fail. This may be why others like him, if they exist, have so far not succeeded—and indeed perhaps never will. A terrorist would understand, however, that the odds are not impossible. He would of course have many concerns as he moved ahead, particularly with transport of an assembled device, and the selection of a city to hit. Does he fly it to the target in a chartered airplane? Does he put it in a container and send it by ship? Does he use the entire ship as a weapon, or does he take the bomb off the ship and truck it to the target? These are important choices, and they would require careful consideration, because each contains risks. But perhaps the obstacles that would least worry a nuclear terrorist are the nominal defenses that have in recent years been erected by Europe and the United States.

THREE

THE WRATH OF KHAN

In reality Washington, London, and New York are unlikely any-time soon to suffer a nuclear strike—though certainly the possibility exists. More at risk for now, it would seem, are the cities of the nuclear-armed poor, particularly on the Indian subcontinent, and in the Middle East. Take Rawalpindi, for instance. For two decades it has stood as it stands today, at the forefront of a new nuclear age—a sprawl of 2 million people on the northern plains of the Punjab, in Pakistan, where already over the past few years the residents have twice come close to nuclear annihilation, yet without losing their enthusiasm for the fact that they, too, have atomic bombs with which to threaten their neighbors. Pacifists may despair and deplore the folly of the masses, but it really hardly matters anymore. Whatever the future may bring, this is the world in which increasingly we live, of societies like Pakistan that are weak and unstable but also nuclear-armed.

Indeed Pakistan is the great proliferator of our time, unlikely though it seems. Rawalpindi is a teeming place almost beyond Western imagination, choked with smoke and overcrowded with people just barely getting by. A large number of them live hand to mouth on the equivalent of a few hundred dollars a year. Much of their drinking water comes from a lake in the peaceful countryside north of town. The lake is surrounded by tree-lined pastures and patches of sparse forest. The navy of Pakistan has a sailing club there, on a promontory with a cinder-block shack, a dock, and one small sloop in the water—a Laser 16 with dirty sails, which sees little use. Though fishermen and picnickers sometimes appear in the afternoons or evenings, the lakefront on both sides of the promontory is pristine and undeveloped. The emptiness is by design: though the land around the lake is privately owned, zoning laws strictly forbid construction there, to protect Rawalpindi's citizens from the contamination that would otherwise result. This seems only right. If Pakistan can do nothing else for its people, it might at least prevent the rich from draining their sewage into the mouths of the poor.

But Pakistan is a country corrupted to its core, and some years ago a large weekend house was built in blatant disregard of the law, about a mile from the navy's sailing club, clearly in sight on the lake's far shore. When ordinary people build illegal houses in Pakistan, the government's response is unambiguous and swift: backed by soldiers or the police, bulldozers come in and knock the structures down. The builder of this particular house, however, was none other than Dr. Abdul Qadeer Khan, the metallurgist who after a stint in Europe had returned to Pakistan in the mid-1970s with stolen designs and had over the years provided the country—single-handedly, it was widely believed—with an arsenal of nuclear weapons. Though he worked in the realm of state secrets, he had become something of a demigod in Pakistan, with a public reputation second only to that of the nation's founder, Mohammed Ali Jinnah, and he had developed an ego to match. He was the head of a government facility named after him—the Khan Research Laboratories, or KRL—which had mastered the difficulties of producing highly enriched uranium, the fissionable material necessary for Pakistan's weapons, and was also involved in the design of the warheads and the missiles to deliver them. The enemy was India, where Khan, like most Pakistanis of his generation, had been born, and against which Pakistan has fought four losing wars since its birth, in 1947. India had the bomb, and now Pakistan did, too. A. Q. Khan was seen to have assured the nation's survival, and indeed he probably has— up until the moment, someday in a conceivable future, when it melts away for other reasons, or when a nuclear exchange actually occurs.

In any case, by the time he built the house on the lake, he believed wholeheartedly in his own greatness. In his middle age he had become a fleshy, banquet-fed man, unused to criticism and outrageously self-satisfied. Accompanied by his security detail, he went around Pakistan accepting awards and words of praise, passing out pictures of himself, and holding forth on diverse subjects—science, education, health, history, world politics, poetry, and (his favorite) the magnitude of his achievements. As befits such a benefactor, he also gave out money, of which he seemed to have an unlimited supply, despite the obvious fact that he was a government official with a government official's salary and no legitimate sources of wealth; he bought houses for his friends, funded scholarships, set up his own private charity, made large donations to mosques, and bestowed grants on Pakistani schools and institutions, many of which duly named themselves or their buildings after him. To understand Khan correctly—which is to anticipate the further spread of nuclear arsenals beyond the traditional powers—it is necessary to recognize that his largesse was not merely a matter of self-aggrandizement. He has been portrayed in the West as a twisted character, an evil scientist, a purveyor of death. He had certainly lost perspective on himself. But the truth is that he was a good husband and father and friend, and he gave large gifts because in essence he was an openhearted and charitable man.

As to why, therefore, he insisted on building a weekend house that drained into Rawalpindi's drinking water, the answer is indeed twisted, though in a standard Pakistani way: the attraction was not in the setting on the lake (there are prettier lakes nearby), but, rather, in the open defiance of the law—an opportunity for the display of personal power. In a country whose courts have been made captive, and whose most fundamental laws have been systematically ignored by corrupt civilian governments and military regimes, once wealth has been achieved there can be no more gratifying display of success than such a brazen illegal act. Khan's house on the lake served as a barely coded message—and one that was universally understood by Pakistanis at the time. It was a public brag. People did not disapprove of Khan for his violation of the law. Even in Rawalpindi they tended rather to admire him for it. They were poor, but collectively no longer weak, because now they had the atomic bomb. They were perfectly willing to make exceptions for the man who had given it to them.

It remained illegal to build on the lake, and as a result, by twisted logic, the restricted property there became some of the most sought-after in the region. A. Q. Khan had pioneered the ground. Within a few years other houses had been built near his, perhaps a dozen in all, and each for the same reason—because of the influence it took to get away with such a public crime. Some of the builders were generals. Some were high-ranking officials from the nuclear laboratory. All of them derived additional glory from their proximity to the beloved Khan.

Then for Khan, in January of 2004, the good life came crashing down. He was sixty-eight at the time. U.S. agents had intercepted a German ship named the *BBC China* carrying parts for a Libyan nuclear-weapons-production program, and Libya, in subsequently renouncing its nuclear ambitions, had named Pakistan, and particularly the Khan Research Laboratories, as the supplier of what was to be a complete store-bought nuclear-weapons program. The price tag was said to be $100 million. At about the same time, it was revealed that the Pakistani-run network had sold information and nuclear-weapons components to Iran and North Korea and had begun negotiations with a fourth country, perhaps Syria or Saudi Arabia. The dictator of Pakistan, General Pervez Musharraf, denied any personal knowledge or governmental involvement and, with his paymasters in Washington, D.C., looking sternly on, accused Khan of running a rogue operation, outside the law. It was theater of the diplomatic kind, and all the more grand because Musharraf controlled an arsenal of atomic bombs. To refrain from using such an arsenal confers automatic gravitas on national leaders, who can stand shoulder to shoulder with similarly equipped presidents and prime ministers, showing restraint and peaceful intent. But Musharraf was an unconvincing actor. A. Q. Khan was a hero not just in Pakistan, but throughout the Islamic world and beyond. For years he had openly represented the right of the global underclass to bear nuclear arms and had indeed publicly advertised the sale of Pakistan's nuclear wares. When Musharraf claimed ignorance and disapproval, he might as well have been expressing surprise that Khan had built a house on the shores of a drinking-water supply.

Still, the theater continued. Khan's top lieutenants had already been detained. Now Khan himself was arrested—taken away by plainclothes security agents who came in the night and drove him to a secret location for a few days of questioning and persuasion. An agreement was reached, and on February 4, 2004, in a stage-managed event, Khan appeared on television and made a public confession in which he apologized to the nation for his behavior and absolved the military regime of involvement. Musharraf called Khan a national hero for his earlier work, then pardoned him and confined him to house arrest at his grand Los Angeles–style residence in the nation's tightly controlled capital, Islamabad, a short drive north of Rawalpindi. Khan has been there ever since, in isolation with his European wife, surrounded by guards and security agents, cut off from contact with the outside world, not allowed to read the newspapers or watch television, let alone to use the telephone or the Internet, and held beyond the reach of even the intelligence services of the United States. The intelligence services would like to question him because of the likelihood that much of the network he established remains alive worldwide, and that by its very nature—loose, unstructured, technically specialized, determinedly amoral—it is both resilient and mutable and can resume its activities when the opportunity arises, as inevitably it will. Pakistan mounted its own investigation and parceled out some information to the United Nations' International Atomic Energy Agency, the IAEA, in Vienna. But for obvious reasons the Pakistani regime could not allow deep scrutiny to occur, and neither, out of perceived geopolitical necessity, could the leaders of the United States.

Khan therefore remains an enigma—a man who may die in isolation, still carrying his secrets with him. Some news does filter out about the conditions of his captivity. He has aged considerably and has lost weight and sickened, but apparently he is not being poisoned. After decades of soft living he suffers from various physical ailments, including chronic high blood pressure, and prostate cancer, for which he underwent surgery in September 2006. He is also deeply despondent—convinced that he served his nation honorably, and that even as he transferred its nuclear secrets to other countries, he was acting on behalf of Pakistan, and with the complicity of its military rulers. He sleeps poorly at night.

Last spring he managed to slip a note out to one of his former lieutenants. It was a scribbled lament in which he asked about General Musharraf, "Why is this boy doing this to me?"

The answer seems obvious: it is a requirement for avoiding American sanctions, and for maintaining power. Ordinary Pakistanis remain on Khan's side, but out of self-protection the elites must turn away from him now.

His longtime scribe, a journalist named Zahid Malik, who for years praised Khan in public and published an adoring biography of him in 1992, told me recently in Islamabad that Khan's arrest was necessary. We met in Malik's office, at a newspaper he founded, called the *Pakistan Observer*. He emphasized his loyalty to the military regime. He said, "After 9/11 Pakistan has emerged as a trusted and responsible ally of the West. Pakistan has adopted a principled position, you see, of working against terrorism, extremism, Al Qaeda, and all that. When Pakistan came to know of certain complaints, Pakistan reacted, you see, and very forcefully. Because as President Musharraf has been saying, and rightly so, whatever Dr. Khan did was his personal act."

He also said that Musharraf is rooting out corruption.

Since we were on the subject of law, I asked him what he

knew about the formal basis for Khan's continuing detention. He did not directly answer. He said, "The government says it is because of his security. His own safety."

I asked, "Do you believe that yourself? That it's in his interest to be confined?"

Malik did not hesitate. Almost eagerly he said, "I think so, I think so."

In Pakistan it pays to be politically realistic. Khan's days on the lake are over, but other people are still out there building or expanding their houses. The most noticeable place is next door to Khan's. It is showy in the style of an international hotel. Khan's house by comparison seems modest now, all the more so because it is shuttered and abandoned. Even on sun-filled days there is a sadness to the scene; in the afternoons when the wind comes up, there is nonetheless a stillness. Khan's garden, which slopes to the shore and was once his pride, is growing wild. He has a little speedboat beside a private dock, but it is open to the rain and is slowly swamping, settling nose-down. No doubt this was to be expected. Khan is the greatest nuclear proliferator of all time. He was a revolutionary of historic significance, and, as is often the case, he was consumed by his own creation. By then his greatest work had been done. Publicly he is disapproved of by governments and the press, but privately people still hold him high. In much of the world they continue to think Long Live Khan, and they probably will for a long time.

Khan's personal history is obscured as much by adulation as by secrecy. Something is known of his childhood. He was born in 1936, to a Muslim family in Bhopal, India—a city now known for the eighteen thousand deaths caused there by an accidental venting, one night in 1984, at a Union Carbide insecticide plant. Bhopal in the 1930s was split between Hindus and Muslims. The two groups lived in wary but peaceful proximity, despite growing religious animosity elsewhere on the subcontinent. Khan was one of seven children. His father was a retired schoolmaster of modest means, with a thin, severe face, a white beard, and a turban. He was a partisan of the Muslim League and, when visiting the bazaar, would warn like-minded men of Mahatma Gandhi's craftiness, and his ambition to annihilate the Muslims. These were common fears at the time, and they were reflected on the Hindu side as well. After World War II, as Great Britain rushed to withdraw from its burdensome colonial charge, and India's factions deadlocked over a power-sharing arrangement, a partition was decided upon that would carve a separate Muslim nation, called Pakistan, from Indian soil. The new nation would itself be split in two, between the Muslim-majority area of the west, primarily along the Indus River, and a smaller Muslim area far to the east, on the delta of the Ganges, in Bengal. It was an awkward exit strategy, but better than trying to control a full-blown civil war. A British official was sent from London, and with no previous expertise in the region, he drew up the boundaries within a few weeks.

Khan by then was a schoolboy, and according to Zahid Malik, he was a perfect one. He was devout, studious, and respectful of his teachers, and for good measure he was also a perfect son. All this and more, Malik believes, had been foretold. He writes that some months after Khan's birth his mother took the infant to a fortune-teller, known as the Maharaj, to look into his future. After performing calculations the Maharaj said, "The birth of this child will bring good fortune to his family. The child is very lucky.

He is going to do a lot of good deeds in his life ahead. He will receive two kinds of education."

In the book Malik pauses to explain, "Probably the Maharaj referred to the Science of Metallurgy and Nuclear Physics, or perhaps to a local and foreign education system."

The fortune-teller continued, "Up to the age of eight months, he will suffer from stomach pain and a cough, after which he will have a long and healthy life. He will outstand in his family and will be a source of great pride and honor to his parents, brothers, and sisters. He is going to do very important and useful work for his nation and will earn immense respect." Furthermore, "Due to your son's good luck, you will soon be rewarded with great wealth."

But first there were troubles to endure. At the time of the Partition, in 1947, one of the greatest migrations in human history got under way, as over a few months more than 10 million people—Hindus, Sikhs, and Muslims—fled the hostility of their old communities and sorted themselves out in the new nations. They moved by train and bus, and on foot. In the absence of governmental power India's social hatreds took form, and the migrants were attacked by mobs. The history is obscure and highly propagandized, but it seems that entire trainloads were massacred on both sides, that rape was rampant, and that several hundred thousand people died. In Pakistan perhaps 7 million Muslims arrived, however traumatized.

A. Q. Khan was not initially among them: his parents chose to remain in Bhopal, where their lives seemed comfortable enough. But the city was no longer really their home, and over the subsequent few years its Muslim residents endured increasing harassment by their Hindu neighbors and the Hindu police. Three of

Khan's older brothers and one of his sisters eventually left for Pakistan, and in the summer of 1952, having passed his matriculation exam, A.Q., at the age of sixteen, followed them there. He traveled across India by train, among a group of other Bhopali Muslims, who were intimidated and attacked by Hindu railroad officials and the police. Jewelry and money were stolen from his companions, and people were beaten. Khan lost merely a pen, but the bullying marked him for life.

The train ride ended at the border town of Munabao, beyond which lay a five-mile stretch of barren desert, and Pakistan. Zahid Malik describes Khan's crossing in the style of a founding epic. Carrying his shoes and a few books and belongings, the young A.Q. walked barefoot across the blistering sands to arrive at last in the Promised Land. He went to live with one of his brothers in Karachi. His mother arrived soon afterward. His father stayed in Bhopal and died there some years later. Khan enrolled at the D. J. Science College of Karachi, where he excelled.

Pakistan by then was five years old. It was still a democracy, albeit a messy one. It had already fought and lost its first war with India over the disputed territory of Kashmir, a mountainous and predominantly Muslim region, which for complex political reasons went to India at the time of the Partition. Pakistan had drawn the wrong lessons from its battlefield loss. It was born a poor nation and could not afford war, but its people hated India, and its military was on the rise. In 1958, on the pretext of threats to the nation, the army of Pakistan overthrew the democratic government and declared martial law. It is not known how Khan reacted. He was twenty-two, and in his final years at a college in Karachi. He believed, as many Pakistanis still do, that India had never accepted the subcontinent's partition, and (as he told his friends) that Hindus were tricksters with hegemonic designs. It is possible, therefore, that he accepted the need for firm leadership. In later years he argued publicly against military rule despite providing Pakistan's generals with the ultimate weapon and, along with that weapon, increased arrogance and strength. But in 1958 he was still essentially an apolitical young man, intent on studying science.

Khan graduated from college in 1960, and at the age of twenty-four became an inspector of weights and measures in Karachi. It was the sort of government job that might have lasted a lifetime, but Khan was more ambitious and secured the funding to pursue his education abroad. In 1961 he resigned from his job and flew to West Berlin to study metallurgical engineering at a technical university there. His German grew fluent. He was lonely for Pakistan, but open to the experience of living in Europe, and to making new friends.

In 1962, while on vacation in The Hague, he met the woman who would become his wife. He had written a postcard home, and when he inquired about the price of a stamp, she was the stranger who happened by with an answer. She was a frumpy-looking girl of twenty, in glasses, by the name of Henny. She had been born in South Africa to Dutch expatriates, and had spent her childhood in Africa before returning with her family to the Netherlands. She held a British passport, and though she spoke native Dutch, she lived in Holland as a registered foreigner. She and Khan corresponded for a few months, after which she took a job in Berlin to be closer to him. After a year they returned to Holland, where Khan transferred to a university in Delft to continue his studies in metallurgy. In 1963 he and Henny were married in a modest Muslim ceremony at Pakistan's embassy in The Hague. The marriage was performed by an embassy official and witnessed by the ambassador, as a standard service to citizens abroad. There was a small tea party, as was usual. Khan had no special connections to the Pakistani government and was not yet working as its spy.

Nonetheless, he was making university contacts in the fields of engineering and applied science and unintentionally laying the foundation for the European network that would help Pakistan to produce nuclear arms. Khan spent four years in Delft, where he earned a master's degree and learned to speak good Dutch. He and Henny then moved to Leuven, in Belgium, where he pursued doctoral studies at Catholic University under a professor named Martin Brabers—a metallurgist who was later to serve (innocently, he claimed) as an important consultant to the Pakistani nuclear-weapons program. In Belgium, Henny gave birth to two daughters, two years apart. Khan said that he did not need a son, and that given the overcrowding of the world, two children were enough. He was not a brilliant researcher but a willing and hardworking one. During his studies in Delft and Leuven he published twenty-three papers and edited one book (with Brabers) on a variety of arcane metallurgical topics. His superiors were impressed, and so were his friends. To top it off, he was affable and outgoing and, as everyone agreed, just a nice guy.

In 1972 Khan received his Ph.D. in metallurgical engineering and, having cast about for jobs, went to work in Amsterdam for an engineering consulting firm called Fysisch Dynamisch Onderzoek, or FDO. He might just as soon have joined a university, a steel mill, or an aircraft manufacturer, because he was certainly not setting out to build a bomb. He was an expert in certain high-strength alloys and perfectly satisfied to remain just that. He was satisfied to have a job. FDO, however, happened to specialize in the design of ultracentrifuges—rapidly spinning tubes that are used to separate and concentrate certain isotopes in gasified uranium, ultimately to produce enriched uranium. In a world without nuclear secrets the enrichment of uranium is nonetheless a particularly difficult process to master, and an area in which practical expertise is of special value to nuclear aspirants. But the people at FDO had no links to weapons of any kind; their main business was to offer the best possible centrifuge designs to a consortium called Urenco (for Uranium Enrichment Company), which had two years before been founded jointly by the governments of Holland, Germany, and Britain to provide fuel to the nuclear-power industry.

With FDO's help, Urenco had built a large state-of-the-art centrifuge plant in the Dutch town of Almelo, on the border with Germany, about an hour's drive from Amsterdam. The process there in broad strokes is not difficult to understand. The fissionable isotope known as U-235 exists in natural uranium at a concentration of only 0.7 percent; for the purposes of a power-generation reactor the concentration of that isotope has to be increased about fivefold, to at least 3 percent; the trick is to isolate and shed a similar isotope known as U-238, which is infinitesimally heavier. By spinning at high speeds—electrically driven to seventy thousand revolutions per minute, in perfect balance, on superb bearings, in a vacuum, linked by pipes to thousands of other units doing the same—this is what the centrifuge achieves. Natural uranium is converted to gas and fed through a "cascade" of spinning centrifuges that incrementally enrich it as it flows. When the desired concentration of U-235 is achieved, the gas is reconverted into a solid metal form, now suitable to fuel nuclear reactions. At Urenco the intent was completely peaceful. The enriched uranium produced at the Almelo plant was relatively tame stuff, designed for the slow burns necessary to heat the water and spin the turbines inside nuclear-power plants. One problem, however, with enrichment technology is that the switch to a military purpose requires hardly more than a shift of the mind. Tangibly, once they were designed, installed, and spinning, the type of centrifuges in use at Urenco were (and are) perfectly capable of continuing the enrichment past the commercial mark, and of concentrating the U-235 to more than 90 percent, which is the threshold necessary for a fission bomb. Indeed if your purpose from the start was to build a nuclear arsenal, you would use the very same machines and simply allow the cascade to function longer. In the end you would have weapons-grade material just like the highly enriched uranium that destroyed Hiroshima—a lump of dull gray metal around which competent machinists could build an atomic bomb.

If at Urenco and FDO the danger seemed far removed from daily life, it was nonetheless accepted as an abstract truth. Even the janitors knew that they were working on the leading edge of a technology that could be used to pulverize cities and tear apart the sky. As a result, the operational details at both companies were held as state secrets, and Khan—like other employees—needed a security clearance before going to work there. This turned out not to be an obstacle. The Dutch internal security service ran a background check, and Khan was approved. Much has been made of this since then, as if the background check were too perfunctory; but Khan had strong references and a clean record, and even he did not yet know what was soon to be on his mind. He was thirty-six years old, a diligent husband, and the father of two. He moved with his family into a nice little house in a nice little town and settled in to enjoy a quiet Dutch life.

Then history came chasing Khan down. As so often, it took the form of war. In the spring of 1971, after years of discriminatory treatment by Pakistan's dominant west, East Pakistan had risen up in rebellion and had begun to agitate for independence as a new nation, called Bangladesh. The Pakistan military reacted brutally, and a ruthless civil war broke out on the Bengali deltas and plains. The fighting went on inconclusively for most of the year, generating huge casualties among civilians and sending several million refugees streaming across the border into India. Pakistan's international reputation, which was never high, sank to an all-time low. Having gauged the geopolitical effect of this correctly, and emboldened by its friendship with the Soviet Union, India then seized the opportunity to dismember its foe and mounted a full-scale invasion of East Pakistan with overwhelming force. The battles were short. Pakistan's once strutting army collapsed, and in December of 1971, at a humiliating ceremony in a stadium in Dacca, it unconditionally surrendered. Ninety-three thousand Pakistani soldiers were taken prisoner. For what it's worth, an independent Bangladesh was born.

Decades later it may seem obvious that the loss of Bangladesh was a blessing, but it is still viewed as a curse in Pakistan today, and it was certainly seen that way at the time. The trauma was severe. The military regime fell, and Pakistan's greatest civilian leader—the democratically elected, populist, and some would say demagogic Zulfikar Ali Bhutto—assumed power. Bhutto was a visionary and seems truly to have believed that he had been born to save the nation. The lessons he drew from the defeat were similar to those of almost all Pakistanis, and therefore probably to those of A. Q. Khan as well. Khan was still in Leuven, wrapping up his dissertation, but with a close eye on the homeland. For a while Pakistan was introspective and self-critical, but no sooner had the domestic purges been completed than the blame for Bangladesh shifted to the outside. A fifth of Pakistan's territory and more than half its population had been lost—and to crafty Hindus, who now seemed certain to want to finish off the rest. To make matters worse, Pakistan in its time of need had been abandoned by its important allies, China and the United States, whose power had been checked by the Soviet Union, and whose nuclear weapons had proved to be of no value at all. Only the Islamic nations had rallied to Pakistan's side, but as a group they were weak and disdained, and incapable of providing much beyond symbolic help. When all was said and done, twenty-four years after the Partition, Pakistan appeared to be in mortal danger and could quite obviously rely on no one but itself. Seen from the vantage point today of a post–Cold War world, the conclusions drawn in Pakistan seem like a harbinger of modern times.

What Khan may not have known, but Bhutto certainly did, was that India had drawn similar conclusions and was well on its way to possessing atomic bombs. The intention to acquire them apparently dated back to before the Partition, when Jawaharlal Nehru, looking forward to independence, said, "I hope Indian scientists will use the atomic force for constructive purposes, but if India is threatened, she will inevitably try to defend herself by all means at her disposal." In the literature on nuclear proliferation today, positions are staked out to explain why nations choose to develop nuclear weapons. Is it because of external threat and strategic defense? International prestige and diplomatic power? Bureaucratic striving? Populism, nationalism, and the need to impress constituents on the streets? In India it seems to have been all of the above, with added emphasis on strategic defense

after India's humiliating 1962 defeat by China and China's subsequent test of a nuclear weapon in 1964. India's program was
pursued in semisecret, closely linked to a public program of
nuclear-power generation and partially masked by it: it would not
use enriched uranium as the fuel for its weapons but rather
would build them around cores made of plutonium, a by-product
of uranium reactors that can be chemically extracted from their
radioactive wastes. On the receiving end the difference between
enriched uranium and plutonium would not matter: the former
had been used against Hiroshima, the latter against Nagasaki,
and either material suitably compressed in a few fission bombs
could release enough energy to devastate Pakistan. Pakistan
protested in capitals around the world and asked for diplomatic
intervention, but to no avail. Though the existence of an Indian
nuclear military program was evident, no sanctions were imposed;
and indeed, Canada, France, and the United States continued to
help India with its nominally peaceful nuclear-power-plant plans.

Pakistan had its own nuclear-power-plant plans, though less
well developed. In the 1950s President Dwight D. Eisenhower
had launched a since discredited program called Atoms for
Peace, under which a benevolent United States, while ensuring
world peace with its rapidly growing nuclear arsenal, would assist
governments with technology and training in the development of
nuclear-power generation—as if such capacities were unrelated
to the development of atomic bombs. Pakistan answered with the
creation of the Pakistan Atomic Energy Commission, known as
the PAEC, which initially had little interest in weapons and, to
the extent that it progressed at all, did indeed concentrate on the
possibilities for electric-power generation. By the mid-1960s,
however, influential Pakistanis had begun to argue for nuclear

deterrence against India. Bhutto, who was then the foreign minister, uttered the now famous remark that Pakistanis would eat grass if necessary, but they would have their bomb.

Given the desperate circumstances of Bhutto's rise to the office of prime minister, in 1971, it is not surprising that he set out almost immediately to make those dreams come true. One month after the surrender of Pakistan's army in Bangladesh, he called a secret meeting of about seventy Pakistani scientists under an awning on a lawn in a town in the Punjab and asked them for a nuclear bomb. He did not mean just one, of course: he was looking for an entire arsenal, and, more important, for the start-to-finish capacity to produce it. Though some dissenters questioned the wisdom of this path, for the most part the assembled scientists responded enthusiastically—and indeed promised delivery within an impossible five years.

As usual the biggest problem they faced was not the design of the bombs, but the acquisition of the fissionable material necessary to fuel them. To manage the project, Bhutto turned to the PAEC, which he placed under a new chairman—an American-trained nuclear engineer named Munir Ahmed Khan, who had for thirteen years been working for the International Atomic Energy Agency, the IAEA, in Vienna. Munir Ahmed Khan was not related to A. Q. Khan and would eventually become his enemy, but at this point the two did not know each other. With no facilities available in Pakistan for the enrichment of uranium, Munir Khan and the PAEC set off in 1971, as the Indians had, to build a plutonium bomb. They planned to extract the plutonium secretly from the radioactive waste of a small Canadian-built power-generation reactor that was just coming online. Though Pakistan was not a signatory to international nonproliferation accords, which would have included oversight of fissile materials as the price for assistance in developing a nuclear-power industry, the Canadians had required that their reactor be placed under IAEA controls: its fuel was to be accounted for before and after use, to verify that none was being diverted or chemically altered. Given his familiarity with the IAEA, however, Munir Ahmed Khan was not unduly concerned. Presumably he believed that the controls would be sufficiently lax, or that Pakistan could somehow secretly acquire additional fuel to feed through the reactor. His main need, therefore, was for a plutonium-extraction plant—a facility that the French eventually agreed to provide.

There is no evidence that A. Q. Khan, now at the consulting firm FDO in Amsterdam, was yet aware of the nuclear escalation on the Indian subcontinent. But on May 18, 1974, an event occurred that left no room for doubt: beneath the desert of Rajasthan, provocatively close to the Pakistani border, India detonated a plutonium-based fission device of roughly the same yield as the uranium bomb that had destroyed Hiroshima. Indian prime minister Indira Gandhi was watching. The desert floor heaved, and a coded message of success was sent to the capital, New Delhi. It read, "The Buddha is smiling." India explained to the world that this had been a peaceful test and asserted that a nuclear device is no more inherently threatening than any other explosive—that the character of a device depends on its intended use. India, you see, is a peaceful nation. The world was unconvinced, but did little in response.

Far away in Amsterdam, A. Q. Khan believed that the Buddha had smiled in anticipation of Pakistan's destruction. He had been working at FDO for two years, and with his access to the Urenco centrifuge technology, he realized he was in a position to help Pakistan face the threat. Apparently on his own, he decided to take action. It is said that soon after the Indian test he sought out a couple of senior Pakistani engineers who were visiting Holland to buy a wind tunnel, but when he mentioned his background and expressed his desire to return to Pakistan to help develop its nuclear capabilities, they discouraged him, saying that his expertise would not be appreciated, and he might not even be able to find a job. That particular story is typical of those Khan later told, with increasing rancor, after he came to see himself in the heroic third person, as the national savior, struggling against the dangerous complacency of others. But the story is plausible enough perhaps to be true.

Khan was not the sort to give up. In the summer of 1974 he sent a letter to Prime Minister Bhutto, presenting his credentials, summarizing the potential of centrifuges, and again volunteering his services. Bhutto responded through the embassy in The Hague. The two men met in Karachi in December of 1974, after Khan and his young family arrived for a holiday. Khan argued for a Pakistani effort to enrich uranium—a route to the bomb, he assured Bhutto, that would be faster than Munir Khan's pursuit of plutonium reprocessing, then under way. The plutonium project was in trouble nearly from the start because the Canadians had responded to the Indian nuclear test, paradoxically, by beginning to withdraw their support for their reactor in Pakistan. The government of Pakistan had expressed its outrage with the Canadian actions, but could not escape Bhutto's having publicly renewed his call for an atomic bomb. Munir Khan and his engineers at the PAEC assured Bhutto that they could run the new reactor without Canadian assistance, and they insisted that with the French plutonium-extraction plant in the offing, Pakistan should stick with its original plan. Bhutto did not disagree, but he saw the advantage of mounting a parallel effort toward enriched uranium and decided on the spot to place A. Q. Khan in charge.

And Khan was a self-starter. Even before the go-ahead from Bhutto, he had gotten to work. For sixteen fruitful days in the fall of 1974 he had stayed in Almelo on a special assignment to Urenco, where he had helped with the translation of secret centrifuge plans from German into Dutch and had, in his spare time, strolled freely through the buildings, among the centrifuges and into offices, taking copious notes in Urdu. Some of the places he had visited were nominally off-limits to him, but not once had he been challenged. A few people had asked him what his notes were about, and he had answered, half-truthfully, that he was writing letters home.

After his conversation with Bhutto in Pakistan, Khan returned to Amsterdam to gather more information. It was early 1975. He was thirty-eight years old and much liked at FDO. As was his habit, he arrived at the lab with postcards, sweets, and other little presents for the staff. Despite the secrets held at FDO, the atmosphere there was even more open and relaxed than at Urenco, with no visible security and none of the culture of suspicion that governments might have wished to impose. One bin held discarded prototype centrifuge parts—components that were perhaps not quite within specifications. Employees were free to scavenge keepsakes from it to display on their desks. Khan now began not merely to scavenge the centrifuge parts, but to take them home. Presumably, some of those components made their way to Pakistan's embassy, which had received instructions from Islamabad to help.

Thirty years later I met Khan's office-mate of 1975, an FDO machinist named Frits Veerman, now sixty-two, who drove me to Almelo, on his first return to the Urenco centrifuge plant in all this time. Veerman turned out to be a typically law-abiding Dutchman with a maddening manner as a driver of strictly respecting the speed limits, even on four-lane roads with no traffic ahead. Riding with him was a rare form of torture not yet known to Pakistan. I soon understood that living with him would have been worse: his wife and children believed he was obsessed with Khan, and they wished he would leave the subject alone. But Veerman had been marked by Khan's actions, and whether because of this brush with fame or because he was truly troubled by the spread of nuclear weapons, he could not stop repeating the story.

He told me that he and Khan had been close friends. They were fellow geeks, I suppose—at least to the extent that centrifuges seem truly to have excited them both. Whenever Khan discovered something interesting on the FDO laboratory floor, or Veerman did, they would troop off together to study it and share their joy. They shared other enthusiasms as well. When the weather turned warm and women in Amsterdam took to walking around in scanty clothes, the two friends would go sightseeing through the city, in earnest appreciation of the female form. Khan in particular was easily smitten and would occasionally wander off on the trail of a woman despite Veerman's entreaties to return to work. I asked Veerman if he meant to say that Khan had frequented prostitutes. He answered as he often did to my questions about those times, with a bewildered and plaintive "I don't know!"—as if he couldn't be sure of anything anymore.

But Khan was almost certainly a good family man, and for that reason a better spy. Veerman was still a bachelor then and was sometimes invited over for dinner. Henny was less gregarious than Khan, and a bit overshadowed by him, but she was gracious and polite, and the two girls were young and nice. The family spoke English at home. Veerman would arrive at the house carrying ten pounds of cheese, or more, because some of his relatives were traditional Dutch cheese makers, and Henny had a special fondness for this stuff. The meals typically consisted of barbecued chicken and rice. Khan had a special fondness for Dutch chicken, which he believed was better than any he had eaten in Pakistan.

The drinks were nonalcoholic. The curtains were left open at night in the style of righteous Dutch towns, and the illumination was kept high so anyone passing on the street could see that inside the house everything was just right. Veerman believed nearly the same for a while, though on several occasions he noticed classified documents on a desk in Khan's home, in apparent violation of the lab's security procedures. Khan once explained that Henny was helping with translations. He was so clearly unconcerned with hiding the documents that Veerman assumed Henny had been checked out and approved and was probably being paid. Sometimes other Pakistanis came for dinner. They did not explain their jobs, and Veerman did not ask. Much later, when Veerman himself was accused of having helped Khan, Dutch intelligence agents showed him photographs of the same men and told him they had come from Pakistan's embassy and were its spies. It appears likely that at the very dinners Veerman enjoyed, blueprints and other documents were collected and taken away. But everything seemed so aboveboard—so normal and brightly lit—that Veerman was mostly just glad to be accepted as a friend. He was probably also proud. The pattern was similar at the lab, where Khan formally and in writing asked Veerman to take detailed photographs of the centrifuges and their parts. Taking photographs was one of Veerman's regular jobs, and because he had a European sense of hierarchy, he unquestioningly complied.

To me, in the car, he said, "Abdul was a doctor, and I was just a normal person—do you understand?"

I said, "Yes," and stifled a sigh.

The story went on, nearly in real time. Finally it was Veerman who suspected that something was wrong about Khan. In those years Veerman liked to vacation in foreign lands, especially when he could lodge with the local people and see life through their eyes. He was not much drawn to Pakistan, but when one day Khan warmly suggested that he should visit and held out the promise that he could stay with Khan's friends and family, Veerman jumped at the chance. Khan suggested places to see and provided Veerman with information about direct flights from London. Veerman began to make his plans.

Khan must have had more than hospitality in mind. Veerman was just some friend from work. Simple though he seemed, he was a highly specialized centrifuge technician, full of useful skills and secret knowledge. In retrospect it is obvious that Khan hoped to tangle him up or seduce him somehow, and to use him in the project to build the Pakistani bomb. The plan might have worked, but then Khan offered to pay for Veerman's flight.

This was an incredible blunder. It is a scientific fact that no other people, anywhere, are as moralistic as the Dutch. Admittedly Pakistan has rather the opposite claim, but Khan had lived in Holland for how long? To state the obvious, Veerman was shocked by Khan's offer, which he immediately declined. He told me that a light lit up in his mind. Khan's wanderings at FDO and Urenco came back to him, as did the classified documents in Khan's home, his mysterious Pakistani guests, the frequent conversations that Khan had conducted in Urdu on his office phone, the photographs he had requested, and his very enthusiasm for centrifuges. Veerman remembered that Khan wore a large gold ring and had once said that if ever he had to flee, he could sell it and get home. It was a joke at the time, but Veerman no longer thought it was funny. What kind of man wears escape on his finger? For that matter, what kind of man could walk away from Holland's gentle embrace? Veerman realized that his friend Abdul was a spy.

Suddenly for Veerman the stakes seemed high. Worried for his own safety, he invented an excuse to cancel the trip to Pakistan and began gingerly to distance himself from Khan. But these were temporary measures at best. Veerman knew that the next time Khan submitted a formal request for photographs, he would have no choice but to disregard it and would have to come up with reasons why. Furthermore, as a man trusted to handle state secrets, he believed that he had a moral responsibility to sound an alarm. The question was how. He had no proof and was intimidated by the idea of making allegations against a man of much higher rank. As best he knew, neither Urenco nor FDO had procedures in place to handle such a case, or to ensure his anonymity.

He tried to ensure it himself. From a public phone, and without identifying himself, he attempted to get through to Urenco's plant director in Almelo. The call was turned away. He tried the same with FDO in Amsterdam, and again he failed. Finally, dropping any attempt at anonymity, he took his concerns in person to his manager at the laboratory. The manager was visibly skeptical, but said he would speak to his superiors. A few days later he sought out Veerman in private and scolded him. He said that such allegations were too serious to be made without proof. He advised Veerman not to stir up trouble at the lab.

FDO was overcome by institutional inertia. Veerman assumed—and still assumes—that nothing was made of his warnings. And Veerman was lucky because Khan did not again ask for photographs. Moreover, the laboratory's unwillingness to confront Khan provided Veerman with the very anonymity he desired: to the end and beyond, Khan never suspected that his friend had betrayed him. But at roughly the same time, the Dutch government learned that a Pakistani agent working out of the embassy in Brussels had attempted to buy a specialized centrifuge component, the knowledge of which seemed perhaps to have come from FDO. Specialized components are rare in the business of building bombs. The Dutch government quietly communicated its concern to the laboratory—with the caveat, however, that the evidence was ambiguous and incomplete. In October of 1975 FDO finally roused itself and promoted Khan to a new and less sensitive job that would keep him away from Urenco's technology. Khan's years in Europe had come to an end. He was never, however, under such pressure that he had to sell his ring and flee. Two months after his promotion, in December of 1975, he simply flew his family back to Pakistan for a Christmas holiday from which he did not return.

Khan had by then succeeded in copying the plans for the most advanced uranium-enrichment process known to the West. Over the decades to come, the Urenco centrifuge design would provide the foundation for Pakistan's nuclear-weapons program, reemerge in the Libyan and North Korean programs, and appear (apparently by independent routes) in Brazil and Iraq as well. It would also move directly from Pakistan to Iran. Such was the appearance of normalcy at the time, however, that neither Urenco nor FDO quite woke up to what had happened. Initially Khan sent word from Pakistan that he had come down with yellow fever and would have to extend his stay into 1976; later he explained that he had found an important new job, and that he would regretfully resign from FDO, effective March 1. Relations remained friendly because Khan showed no tendency to duck and hide. He was narcissistic. Such was his self-centeredness that apparently he felt no regret, even on a personal level, for the trust he had betrayed, and he refused to believe that decent people—for instance, his old friends in Europe—might consider that he had done something wrong.

These attitudes predated his return to Pakistan. He had known enough while at Urenco to lie about the nature of his letters back home, and he must have had some sense that he might be subject to prosecution; but he was an effective spy largely because, for reasons of personality, he was such an open one. The Netherlands and Pakistan were not adversaries, it is important to note, and Khan seems to have felt that he was pursuing a legitimate project that did not affect the Dutch, and in that sense was no one's business but his own. For their part, the managers at FDO remained confused. They knew that Khan was now involved in a large government project in Pakistan, and they must have figured that he was going to build centrifuges. Nonetheless, they continued to communicate with him, and in 1977, having sent a representative to Islamabad, they went so far as to sell him expensive Urenco-style instrumentation. Given the stakes involved, and the possibility of their own ruination, it does not seem that they were motivated by greed. More likely, they were simply sort of sleepy.

Veerman by contrast was wide-awake and nervous. From a distance Khan continued to cultivate him as a source of secret information. In January of 1976 he wrote:

Dear Frits, it is now almost a month since we left the Netherlands, and I am gradually beginning to miss the de-

*licious chicken. Every afternoon I think: ask Frits if he
feels like eating chicken.*

After another chatty letter, in which he extolled the spring
beauty of Islamabad and renewed his invitation to Veerman to
visit, Khan wrote twice again and, this time, got down to business. In one letter, for instance, he wrote:

*Very confidentially, I request you to help us. I urgently
need the following for our research program:*

1. Etches of pivots:

(a) Tension—how many volts?

(b) Electricity—how many amperes?

(c) How long is etching to be done?

*(d) Solution (electrolytic) HCl or something other is
added as an inhibitor.*

*If it is possible, [I would be] grateful for 3–4 etched
pivots. I shall be very grateful if you could send a few negatives for the pattern. You would be having negatives of
these.*

*2. Lower shock absorber. Can you provide a complete
absorber of CNOR? Please give my greetings to Frencken,
and try to get a piece for me. You can ask for it, or get it in
pieces. In any case I shall like to request you very strongly
to send me a few pieces (3 or 4) of membranes, and a few
pieces of steel springs that are used in the absorber. . . .*

*Frits, these are very urgently required, without which
the research would come to a standstill. I am sure you can
provide me with these. These two things are very small,
and I hope you will not disappoint me.*

Veerman did not respond, and instead took the letters to his supervisor at the lab. The supervisor advised him to cut the tie entirely by destroying the letters and warned him that otherwise he might find himself in jail. Veerman angrily disregarded the advice, kept the letters, and continued to push the company to take action—or so he now says. The action finally taken was to fire Veerman, because he was really quite annoying. For a while afterward Veerman was unemployed. During that period he was picked up by Dutch agents who were trudging along belatedly on Khan's trail.

The agents took Veerman to a prison in Amsterdam, where for two days they questioned him. As might be expected, the questioning grew confrontational. The agents accused Veerman of spying, but were no match for him and had to back down in the face of his outrage. He in turn accused them of having made a huge mistake in allowing this technology to escape. And for what, he asked—the financial benefit of a few Dutch companies?

Apparently the agents were a little dull. One said, "You have made trouble."

Veerman answered, "No, *you* have made trouble! I was a technician with a security clearance, and I found a spy in my laboratory!"

"This is not your problem."

"Yes, it is! I have a top security clearance!"

"Go home. You may not talk about this anymore. It is dangerous for Holland. Go home."

Veerman did go home, but he began speaking to local reporters. Word gradually spread, not only of what Khan might have done in Amsterdam but, by logical extension, of what he might be doing now. Veerman remained under surveillance by the Dutch security services for more than a year. Eventually he burrowed into the bureaucracy of a health-insurance company, where he spent the rest of his working life.

Press reports about Khan's spying continued to emerge, and they provoked emotional responses from Khan and his friends, who believed by the late 1970s that a smear campaign had been organized in the West. In 1980 Khan responded to a report in the British *Observer* with a vitriolic letter to the editor, in which he pretended that he was not embarked on a project to built atomic bombs. He wrote:

> *The article on Pakistan in the issue of 9.12, 1979 by Colin Smith and Shyam Bhatia was so vulgar and low that I considered it an insult to reflect on it. It was in short words a bull-shit, full of lies, insinuations and cheap journalism for money and cheap publicity. Shyam Bhatia, a Hindu bastard, could not write anything objective about Pakistan. Both insinuated as if Holland is an atomic bomb manufacturing factory where, instead of cheese balls, you could pick up "triggering mechanisms." Have you for a moment thought of the meaning of this word? Of course not because you could not differentiate between the mouth and the back hole of a donkey.*

The style here was Early Classic Khan, and it indicated a growing problem he had with being discreet. The letter was smoke where there was fire. But despite such obvious prevarication, and the fact that Khan had indeed walked away with sensitive information, under Dutch law it was difficult to prove that Khan had been a spy. In 1980 the Dutch government issued an embarrassed report, concluding that Khan had probably stolen centrifuge designs but pointing out that the evidence remained weak and circumstantial. Three years later after further investigations, when the Dutch finally prosecuted Khan, it was not for espionage but for the letters he had written to Veerman requesting classified information. "Attempted espionage" was the most the prosecutors could convincingly claim. Khan was convicted in absentia and sentenced to four years in prison.

Khan saw dark forces at play. Zahid Malik faithfully writes, "This court was comprised of three judges, and was presided over by a woman who was a Jew. Another of the judges was also a Jew. It looked as if this case was instituted under pressure from the Israeli Prime Minister, and its verdict was also written in Tel Aviv."

If so, the Zionists were uncharacteristically sloppy, because Khan was never properly served with the charges. Two years later, in 1985, a Dutch appeals court overturned his conviction on procedural grounds. Khan appeared on Pakistani television for the first of many times. He said, "This case was false and mala fide. I am happy that it is all over, because my prestige, which had been affected, has now not only been vindicated, but all the allegations which were being leveled against Pakistan's nuclear program have also been quashed." Not even Khan could have quite believed these claims. But Khan was feeling strong, and he could not keep himself from strutting. By then a decade had passed since his return from Holland, and as foreign intelligence services were coming to recognize, Pakistan had in that short time already achieved the capacity to build nuclear bombs. Khan's television appearance therefore was a taunt. Some of the Western powers had arrogantly predicted that in such a place as

Pakistan it could not be done, and Khan—here openly representing all the world's underdeveloped nations—was chortling on camera for having proved the Westerners wrong.

When, someday, the nuclear arming of the poor is nearer to completion—when, say, a few dozen fourth-rate countries have acquired such destructive power—people may still be blaming the Dutch, as they do today, for having allowed Khan to obtain such dangerous knowledge and run away. The truth however is that Khan's thefts in Holland were no more preventable than those of Soviet spies in the United States had been. More profoundly, and as in other famous cases of nuclear espionage, the secrets Khan stole merely provided for some shortcuts on a path that was already well known. Once Bhutto decided to have the bomb, his nation would not be denied. This is just as true for any other determined country—and just as true now for North Korea and Iran. Khan's rapid success came as a particular shock because it so quickly transformed this runt called Pakistan into something like a runt with a gun. But to see that success in depth, and to anticipate the further spread of nuclear weapons, it is insufficient to focus on the loss of state secrets, or to single out the Dutch.

Khan has repeatedly said that the designs he obtained in Holland were not nearly enough. Building the thousands of centrifuges that were necessary, then putting them to use, required solving untold numbers of practical problems, and equipping a new industrial plant with technology that lay beyond the indigenous capabilities of Pakistan. Khan's solution, once he returned to Pakistan, was to buy the technology in bits and pieces from manufacturers and consultants in the West. He knew where to shop because he had kept names and addresses from his years in Europe, and he knew who might provide what, and why. Later he bragged that it was this knowledge, and not his so-called theft of designs, that counted most in enabling Pakistan to build the bomb.

The markets he worked were gray rather than black, because with few exceptions the equipment and materials had multiple uses and would trigger questions only if a nuclear purpose was openly declared. For the most sensitive items Khan used front companies, false end-user certificates, and third-country destinations to obscure the intended use; but generally he or his agents simply went out and bought the stuff. The list was long. Machine tools, magnets, exotic steel. Vacuum pumps, ball bearings, instrumentation of all kinds. The manufacturers who sold to Khan, like the European professors who signed on as his consultants, tended to be willingly naive and greedy. Those who were confronted by Western authorities invariably claimed to believe they were helping an impoverished country to pursue peaceful research.

Pakistan was indeed an impoverished country, and all the more so because it was spending a fortune on this. Nuclear weapons are cheap relative to the destruction they can wreak, but in absolute terms they are expensive nonetheless. I've been told that Khan was willing to pay two or three times the going rate for what he bought, as a premium for working fast and in the shadows. And having such money was fun. Spending it gave Khan power. He felt vindicated somehow that in the same nations where he was being pilloried as a spy, so many people would, as he described them, come begging for his business. Nor did it escape his attention that one of those nations was Pakistan's former colonial master, and that the beggars were whites. At times it was nearly enough to make a man glad for the nuclear success, next door, of all those brown-skinned Hindu bastards.

Khan particularly resented two of the traditional nuclear powers. Responding to criticisms of Pakistan's program, he wrote a
bitter letter in 1979 to the German newsmagazine *Der Spiegel*, in
which he said:

> *I want to question the bloody holier-than-thou attitudes of
> the Americans and the British. Are these bastards God ap-
> pointed guardians of the world to stockpile hundreds of
> thousands of nuclear warheads, and have they God-given
> authority to carry out explosions every month? If we start
> a modest programme, we are the satans, the devils.*

Khan was overstating the numbers, but he was also expressing
an opinion widely held in many countries, and making a legitimate point. Since the 1960s the possession of nuclear weapons
had been considered the exclusive prerogative of the five permanent members of the UN Security Council—the Soviet Union,
France, Great Britain, China, and the United States—with a special exception made for Israel, which has always prudently
denied having acquired the bomb. The inequity of this arrangement was formalized in 1970, when Khan was still a graduate
student in Belgium, by the openly discriminatory Nuclear Non-
Proliferation Treaty, or NPT, which recognized the overlap
between electric-power generation and the construction of
weapons and attempted to place controls on the spread of fissionable fuel and nuclear technology.

The NPT still constitutes the foundation for nonproliferation
efforts worldwide. As the Russian nuclear official recently mentioned to me in Moscow, it was created in the context of the Cold
War's credible guarantees of responses in kind to nuclear aggres-
sion—the umbrellas offered by the Soviet Union and the United

States to Europe and some of their third-world allies. It has four essential parts. The first prohibits the traditional non-nuclear-weapons states (or the 184 that have signed—India, Pakistan, and Israel never have, and North Korea has withdrawn) from attempting to build nuclear weapons. The second assures those same states that as a consequence of joining the treaty they have the right to acquire peaceful nuclear technology—subject, however, to inspections and controls by the United Nations' nuclear agency, the Vienna-based IAEA, to assure that civilian programs are not being exploited for secret military aims. The treaty's structure so far seems reasonable—at least for countries with no immediate intention of building bombs. But the third part, which is an operational understanding, works as a subversive display of just the sort of political advantage that nuclear weapons can provide: it is a blanket exemption from any such international intrusion for the traditional Club of Five. Finally, the fourth part is a feeble promise that the declared nuclear powers will themselves somehow, someday, disarm—standing down from power in a dreamworld without nuclear weapons, which no one has ever realistically expected to see.

In the West the weaknesses of the Non-Proliferation Treaty were understood from the start. For the treaty to have weight it would have to be backed by the threat of sanctions—but even then, given the willingness of countries such as Pakistan (or now Iran) to "eat grass" to acquire such military capabilities, it was unlikely to deter serious aspirants from pursuing the bomb. The solution would, therefore, lie in the complex realm of export controls—a global array of loosely coordinated national laws intended to license and restrict the sale of dual-use materials and components that might appear to be for peaceful purposes (nuclear or non-nuclear) but could be used in the development of a nuclear arsenal. Emphasis was to be placed on technologies that would allow countries to become self-sufficient in nuclear fuels—on uranium-enrichment and plutonium-extraction plants. The export of sensitive items would be allowed to countries that had joined the treaty, subject to IAEA scrutiny on the ground, but would be banned to countries that had refused to sign, such as Pakistan.

The reliance on the United Nations posed obvious operational problems: the IAEA was a politicized bureaucracy, awash in national jealousies, and staffed by nuclear advocates who considered themselves to be in the business primarily of providing this marvelous energy source to the developing world, and not of serving as watchdogs. Nonetheless, in the early and mid-1970s two groups of technologically advanced countries (diplomatic assemblies known as the Zangger Committee and the Nuclear Suppliers Group) began to meet to decide on the lists of restricted materials and equipment and to negotiate the tricky terrain of national implementation and cooperation between participating governments. Over the decades that followed their record was mixed. Though the groups produced ever-longer export-control lists that perhaps helped to slow the nuclear trade by forcing more of it underground, they were stymied by national bureaucracies, slowed by governmental reluctance to interfere with lucrative business deals, and frustrated by the sheer volume of global trade. As a result their work lagged behind the market they intended to regulate. And at no point were they a match for players such as A. Q. Khan.

In fairness to the Western functionaries, however, Khan turned out to be an unusually aggressive man. After his return to Pakistan in December of 1975, he spent a few months within the confines of the Pakistan Atomic Energy Commission, but chafed at the slow pace there. The PAEC had set off in a fairly ponderous bureaucratic style to acquire plutonium; Khan had arrived to pursue the alternative fuel much faster and had almost immediately concluded that the PAEC was intentionally holding him back. Already Khan tended to conflate his own goals with those of the nation, and to interpret personal opposition as something close to treason. He arranged for a private meeting with Prime Minister Bhutto, during which he accused the PAEC chairman, Munir Ahmed Khan, of betraying Pakistan's trust. As he later remembered it to his friends, Khan said, "Munir Ahmed Khan and his people are liars and cheats. They have no love for the country. They are not even faithful to you. They have told you a pack of lies. No work is being carried out, and Munir Ahmed Khan is cheating you." Apparently A. Q. Khan believed that Munir Ahmed Khan had been tainted by his years among the regulators at the IAEA, and that he was actively subverting Pakistan's nuclear program. This was nonsense of course, but an impressive measure of A. Q. Khan's ambitions and energies. Evidently Bhutto was a good judge of men. With nothing to be gained by forcing the two Khans to work together, and with perhaps some benefits to accrue from setting up a competition, he decided to give A. Q. Khan complete autonomy. Khan at that moment knew no bounds. At the age of thirty-nine, he was about to show the entire world what could be done.

On July 31, 1976, Khan founded Engineering Research Laboratories, initially to build and operate a full-scale centrifuge plant based on the stolen Urenco designs. For privacy, he chose a remote site among low, forested hills about forty miles southeast of Islamabad, near a town called Kahuta. The uranium would be mined in central Pakistan, converted to gas, then trucked there to be refined. The stated purpose if anyone asked would be to produce low-enriched fuel for power-generation reactors—albeit beyond international controls. As usual in such countries, what mattered was not the appearance of truth, but pro forma deniability. The plant was to be large, an entire campus of industrial buildings, offices, and living quarters for the staff. Khan started into it immediately and on multiple fronts—hiring staff, laying out the installations, initiating the construction of the most important buildings, and setting up a pilot project elsewhere to resolve the practical problems of building and operating the first centrifuge models. His budget was apparently unlimited. Eventually he hired as many as ten thousand people. He also launched a massive shopping spree in Europe and the United States.

It is obvious that the U.S. government must have known what was going on. Bhutto had made no secret of his ambitions, and by conventional logic it made sense for Pakistan to acquire a nuclear bomb. As an element of Cold War strategy, Pakistan remained a U.S. client state, somewhat prickly under Bhutto, but supported by American aid, and still quite accessible to American diplomats and officials. It is reasonable to assume—and was always presumed within Khan's inner circle to be true—that the CIA had penetrated both the PAEC and Kahuta from an early date. Given the size of the programs under way, this would have been easy to do. The view from the inside must have been sobering indeed: despite the continuing assumption among European governments that the Pakistanis lacked the necessary skills, it became clear that the effort was serious, and that it was likely to succeed. Such an outcome seemed all the more worrisome in Washington, D.C., because Bhutto had resentfully mentioned Christian, Jewish, Hindu, and Communist bombs, and the possibility therefore existed that a Pakistani device would amount to more than a counterbalance to India's weapons—that it would be treated as a "Muslim" bomb to be spread around. Apparently other countries had the same idea, though with hope rather than fear. Libya and Saudi Arabia, for example, are both suspected of having funded Khan early on, probably with the expectation of a return. In any case, by the late 1970s, as Khan proceeded determinedly and U.S. appeals to desist were rebuffed by the government in Islamabad, American officials realized that the only chance they had to stop Pakistan from building a bomb was to take the supply-side approach—to block Pakistan's procurements abroad.

Blocking procurements within the United States proved to be relatively easy because Khan had few American contacts, and domestic U.S. export-control lists were already quite extensive— significantly more so than those that had been agreed upon in the international accords with the other supplier nations. Moreover, deep within the customs and commerce bureaucracies, where day to day such regulations are effectuated or not, American officials, as representatives of a dominant nuclear power, tended just naturally to agree on the importance of nonproliferation and were alert to hints of violations that appeared in the paperwork that crossed their desks. As a result, though some transactions slipped by unseen, the U.S. government thwarted most of the attempted acquisitions from American suppliers. A few companies were fined, but intent was difficult to prove.

The export-control record was altogether different in Europe, where constellations of companies were selling their wares to the Pakistanis, often with the tacit or explicit approval of their governments. In a breathless but generally reliable book titled *The Islamic Bomb*, published in 1981, the reporters Steve Weissman and Herbert Krosney tell a typical story of three of Khan's purchasing agents, who in 1976 went to a small Swiss company in a small Swiss town and proposed to buy its specialized high-vacuum valves for the express purpose of equipping a Pakistani centrifuge enrichment plant. The company dutifully checked with the Swiss authorities, who sent back a printout of their export regulations, including the list of restricted items as defined by the Nuclear Suppliers Group.

Weissman and Krosney write:

> *Complete centrifuge units were listed, and could only be exported to [IAEA] safeguarded facilities, which the Pakistani enrichment plant was not. High-vacuum valves were not listed, even if expressly intended for a centrifuge enrichment unit. The valves might be necessary to the centrifuge, but, in the logic of the . . . list, they were not "nuclear sensitive," and did not directly separate the two different uranium isotopes, uranium 235 and uranium 238.*

In other words, the company was informed that it could proceed with the sale, and so it did—as did others throughout Western Europe. In Holland a company in the automotive-transmission business sold sixty-five hundred high-strength steel tubes to Pakistan—tubes that could serve as the basic components of centrifuges. The Dutch government knew of the deal and advised against it, but the company sent the tubes anyway (initially claiming that they were for irrigation) and argued that no export license was required under Dutch law. Adding to the frustration, it turned out that the company was right. Its argument was accepted, and further shipments went through without delay. Years later the Dutch did finally proceed with some paltry prosecutions, including one that led to the conviction of a Dutch businessman named Henk Slebos for illegally exporting an American-made Tektronix oscilloscope in 1983. Slebos was a personal friend of Khan's, and one of his main European suppliers. He was sentenced to a year in prison, but never served the time and continued brazenly to send equipment to Pakistan. Attention was so lax that Khan himself continued to visit Europe even before his espionage conviction was overturned, in 1985.

Such was the scene that American officials faced in the global nuclear marketplace as they grappled with the inadequacy of the United Nations approach and tried through private entreaties to European governments to prevent the spread of nuclear weapons. They were undercut, as they are today, by the thousands of nuclear warheads that the United States insisted on retaining for itself, and the resentment that such an obvious double standard provoked even during the Cold War, and within countries such as Germany and the Netherlands, which were said to be direct beneficiaries of American nuclear strength. The American officials did experience a few successes—particularly in 1977, when they pressured the French into backing out of the lucrative agreement to provide Munir Ahmed Khan with a long-desired plutonium-reprocessing plant. The French cancellation set back the PAEC's nuclear-weapons plans by a decade or more. This turned out, however, not to matter. Indeed the blow against the PAEC simply served to strengthen A. Q. Khan in his fast-track pursuit of alternative goals.

The truth is that little could be done to dissuade Pakistan from its course—not that the futility of trying provided a compelling reason to abandon the attempt. For France the cost of killing the plutonium deal was several billion dollars, because of the loss of associated contracts for French products such as airplanes and trucks. The decision was all the more difficult because, with its small and independent *force de frappe*, France embodied the right, and perhaps the need, of independent nations to bear nuclear arms. Such was France's ambivalence that it had even refused to join the Non-Proliferation Treaty, although as one of the Club of Five it would have been privileged. (Belatedly, it did finally sign the NPT in 1992, after the end of the Cold War had undermined the meaning of the treaty by weakening the structure of retaliatory assurances on which the theory of nonproliferation was based.) Nonetheless, in 1977, as an established power pretending to diplomatic relevance, France had little choice but to back away from the PAEC once it was faced with evidence of Pakistan's ambitions. By American estimation France this time behaved well.

West Germany, however, did not. Thirty years had elapsed since World War II, the German economy was strong, and the government had embarked on an ambitious program of energy self-sufficiency, which was to be achieved largely through nuclear-power generation. Germany had joined the Non-Proliferation Treaty in 1970, but from the start it had been concerned almost exclusively with the provisions that promoted the rights of member states to acquire peaceful nuclear technology. In practice the German government did not rigorously differentiate between countries that were member states and countries that were not. In the mid-1970s it entered into a major nuclear deal with Brazil, which had not joined the treaty but agreed in this case to accept IAEA safeguards as if it had. Such safeguards were weak, and everyone knew it. Nonetheless, Germany was going to sell Brazil no fewer than eight nuclear reactors, a uranium-enrichment plant, a fuel-fabrication plant, and plutonium-reprocessing facilities. Presumably the centrifuges would be of the same Urenco design that A. Q. Khan was stealing for Pakistan at that very time.

U.S. officials were angry because they had indications that Brazil was secretly seeking a bomb. As was Argentina, which had rejected the Non-Proliferation Treaty as "the disarmament of the disarmed." But when the Americans took their concerns to Bonn, the Germans reacted skeptically and said they would proceed with the deal. An inside observer recently said to me, "The Americans said, 'Hey, wait a minute! This is what we can show you.' And they showed the Germans a little bit of information that indicated Brazil's intention to build a bomb. Apparently it was just enough to persuade the Germans that they were off the reservation." The Germans gave in and reluctantly let the Brazilian contracts drift. Fifteen years later, for domestic political reasons, both Brazil and Argentina formally renounced their nuclear-weapons ambitions—at least for a while.

But the Germans were increasingly restive. Reflecting a sentiment that was widespread in Europe, they resented the disproportionate power of the United States and suspected the Americans of wanting to use the issue of nonproliferation to corner the free-world market in peaceful nuclear fuels. The founding of Urenco was an act of resistance to such perceived domination. Resentment toward the United States was greatest not among the national policymakers, who could sometimes be swayed, but deep within European bureaucracies, among the ordinary diplomats and officials who transacted the daily business of government and were largely immune to American pressure. It was on that level—or lower—that the Pakistani purchasing network operated, and that the American attempts to stop Khan completely failed. The pattern was repetitive. Whenever American intelligence analysts discovered that one company or another was about to export devices to Pakistan, U.S. officials would pass the information along in memos to their European counterparts, expecting that the transactions would be stopped. In some cases the Europeans refused to act because the sales were unambiguously legal. In many other cases, however, interpretation was possible, and with sufficient commitment and energy by government officials the companies could have been approached and warned off. Instead, the Europeans closed ranks. Their attitude toward American officials was them against us. The memos were slid into drawers, and the drawers were slid shut.

In Islamabad, A. Q. Khan was riding high. Such was the perceived importance of his work that he seemed safe from the political dangers even of Pakistan. His mentor Zulfikar Bhutto was overthrown in 1977 and later hanged, but the new dictator, General Zia-ul-Haq, proved to be just as committed to the bomb. By cutting off foreign aid for a year starting in September of 1977, the United States tried forcing Zia to cancel the French plutonium plan, but the effect was only to heighten Pakistan's nuclear resolve. People don't like being pushed around. In April of 1979 the United States tried for a second time, suspending aid because of Pakistan's nuclear activities—but only eight months later, on Christmas Day, the Soviet Union invaded Afghanistan, and suddenly it seemed to Washington that more important issues were at stake. Aid was resumed and nuclear nonproliferation quietly de-emphasized, as over the following decade Pakistan helped to bleed the Soviet Union on behalf of the United States. Much has been written about the folly of that trade-off—and certainly the wisdom of the Afghan war will be argued for years to come—but the truth is that nothing the United States had done or could feasibly do was going to keep Pakistan from acquiring nuclear arms. Then as now, the United States simply lacked the power.

Khan, for one, never doubted his success. As long as he was

granted autonomy and the budget he demanded, he was going to build the bomb. It is believed that as early as 1978 he may have had a prototype centrifuge running and been able to show some increase in the concentration of the isotope U-235. Three years later, in 1981, the production plant at Kahuta was ready to start up, and with such promise that General Zia renamed it the Khan Research Laboratories. This was the sort of gesture that made Khan inordinately proud. The work continued. There were difficulties with balancing the centrifuges, and with earthquakes and floods, but in just a few years Kahuta had perhaps ten thousand centrifuges in place, and already a good number of them were linked into cascades. Around 1982 the plant produced Pakistan's first weapons-grade fuel, a few pounds of uranium enriched to 90 percent or more. By 1984 it was producing enough fissionable material to build several bombs a year. Nor had Khan neglected the need for a weapon that could put this material to use. His bomb was an implosion device, based on a simple Chinese design, with an enriched-uranium core the size of a soccer ball surrounded by a symmetrical array of high explosives wired to a high-voltage switch to be triggered all at once. Soon he was going to work on a missile, too.

But Khan had a problem, and it was sickening his soul. Despite his repeated attempts to discredit Munir Ahmed Khan, the PAEC was still officially heading up Pakistan's nuclear-weapons program. Having been set back by the cancellation of the French extraction plant, it had restarted the quest for a plutonium-reprocessing plant—a goal that would, if achieved, diminish the importance of A. Q. Khan and indeed relegate Kahuta to the position of a mere supplier of enriched uranium in the long production chain necessary to produce plutonium as Pakistan's nuclear-weapons fuel. Equally troubling, the PAEC was designing a missile and was developing its own warhead—one based on plutonium, but otherwise so similar to Kahuta's that A. Q. Khan concluded that the PAEC had stolen his design. Khan fought back with transparent emotion, and increasingly in public. His surrogate Zahid Malik, for instance, published this description of Munir Ahmed Khan:

> *Although some of his loyal friends rank him as a good administrator (or a shrewd manipulator), nobody accepts him as a good scientist. He lacks moral values and is very devious. He can even be cruel where his personal interests are concerned. According to the authors of "The Islamic Bomb," Dr. I. H. Usmani had declared Munir Ahmed Khan a liar and a selfish person who disgraced Pakistan internationally by his conspiracies. According to these authors, he is a treacherous fellow, and time has also shown that he not only cheated Mr. Bhutto but also created a lot of problems for Pakistan in the development of nuclear power and capability. Mr. Goldschmidt, Director General of the French Atomic Energy Commission, said, "I never trusted anything Munir Khan said. He could lie while being charming. I never believed a word that he said."*

But if Pakistan was being disgraced, it was by such crude and childish displays. In what kind of society would the elites consider that such characterizations might seem credible and should be put into print? The conclusion quite obviously is that socially and intellectually Pakistan was an extremely primitive place. This is important to note, because nonetheless Pakistan was capable of rapidly becoming a nuclear-weapons power.

Khan must have known that Bhutto and now Zia were string-

ing him along, and that the rivalry he felt with the PAEC allowed
the political leadership of Pakistan to play him for a fool. But
Khan apparently could not help himself. His ego was inflamed.
He had developed such a need for power and recognition that
there was simply no room for anyone else. It was frustrating to
him that the weapons work at Kahuta was supposed to be secret,
because it meant that he could not shout to the world quite as
loudly as he would have liked. In his interviews and speeches,
which were increasingly frequent, he had a way of insisting that
uranium was being enriched to only 3.5 percent, and purely for
peaceful purposes, but then letting his pride get the best of him
and proceeding at length to discuss the logic and technology of
nuclear weapons. The pattern was strange. In part it stemmed
from a deliberate position of nuclear ambiguity, similar to the
Israeli choice to neither confirm nor deny; but to the extent
that Khan kept talking and talking, it also reflected his personal
needs. He was poor at keeping secrets because he acted too
clever when he lied. He was too eager to claim credit. His denials
were not intended to be believed. What he seemed to be saying
was, We have the bomb, and because of me.

By 1986 Pakistan had crossed the threshold and was able to
fabricate several nuclear devices. It did not announce or test
them, but soon put its new strength to use, when, toward the end
of the year, India mounted a large and threatening military exercise on the plains along Pakistan's borders. The exercise was
dubbed Brasstacks, as in "getting down to . . ." Pakistan responded by mobilizing its own troops, and apparently issued a
veiled nuclear warning. It was contained in an interview that
Khan gave at his house in Islamabad to a freelance Indian reporter. According to the reporter, Khan reiterated earlier boasts
that Pakistan had succeeded in enriching uranium to weapons-

grade levels and added, "Nobody can undo Pakistan, or take us for granted now . . . And let me be clear that we shall use the bomb if our existence is threatened." Publication of the story was delayed for several weeks while the reporter shopped it around, diminishing its immediate effect. Khan later denied having said any such thing, and accused the reporter of being a typical Hindu hack. But in India the message had nonetheless been received, and it would resonate for years to come.

There may have been other messages as well. Despite subsequent Pakistani denials, the Indians claimed that their diplomats heard similar threats at the same time in Islamabad. Furthermore, at the height of the tensions, when the opposing armies stood face-to-face along the border, and India (as is known now) seriously contemplated a preemptive strike, General Zia flew to an Indian-Pakistani cricket match in India, where he sat beside Rajiv Gandhi and, it is alleged, at one point leaned over and said, "If your forces cross our border by an inch, we are going to annihilate your cities." Whether or not he spoke those words, it is widely believed that he did. India soon withdrew its army, and by the time the crisis was over, Pakistan had emerged as a proud new nuclear-weapons state.

Zia died in a mysterious airplane crash in 1988, and Pakistan entered a decade of political turbulence during which it endured various corrupt and incompetent governments, with the army holding real power in the background. For a while in the United States the White House continued to certify to Congress, as it had since the start of the proxy war in Afghanistan, that Pakistan was nuclear-weapons-free. Maintaining that fiction was an annual requirement for providing Pakistan with financial aid. But after the

Soviets withdrew from Afghanistan, in 1989, the fiction no longer seemed necessary, and with concerns about nuclear proliferation again predominating, American aid was cut off. The cutoff saved U.S. taxpayers some money, but it was sapped of moral weight by America's own nuclear stance, and in Pakistan, as usual, it failed to achieve the desired results. For Khan the new sanctions became a point of pride. He had never been particularly religious, but his politics were becoming increasingly Muslim and defiant.

A Pakistani general asked him if he minded the descriptions of him in the West as an evil Dr. Strangelove. Khan answered accurately enough, "They dislike our God. They dislike our Prophet. They dislike our national leaders. And no wonder they dislike anybody who tries to put his country on an independent and self-reliant path. As long as I am sure that I am doing a good job for my country, I will ignore all such insinuations and concentrate on my work."

And concentrate he did. In the face of increasing export controls in the 1990s, Khan did not shy away, but expanded his global procurement network and took it largely underground. At Kahuta he continued to improve the centrifuge plant, to tweak the laboratory's warhead designs, and to develop an alternative ballistic missile to the one being built by the PAEC. He also led the laboratory into the design and manufacture of a variety of conventional weapons, including surface-to-air missiles, anti-tank weapons, multibarrel rocket launchers, laser range-finders, laser sights, reactive armor, minesweeping charges, and armor-piercing tank rounds. On the civilian side Kahuta launched into the manufacture of electronic circuits, industrial switches and power supplies, and compressors for window-mounted air conditioners. In 1992 it even established a Biomedical and Genetic-Engineering Division. Furthermore, it began to hold seminars and conferences on topics related to the enriching of uranium, including six International Symposia on Advanced Materials; two International Symposia on Mechanical Vibrations; the International Conference on Phase Transformations; three Vacuum Courses, some in cooperation with the Pakistan Vacuum Society; and finally, every bomb builder's favorite, the National Conference on Vibrations in Rotating Machinery.

In other words, Khan was going great guns. And he was having fun. Pakistan's nuclear position remained officially ambiguous, but once the American sanctions had been imposed, Khan was freer to praise himself for what he had done. Word filtered through the streets until even ordinary people knew of this grand man, and some recognized him as he whisked by in his cavalcades, surrounded by loyalists and guards. Medals and awards were showered upon him, and every one of them he counted, and every one, he felt, was justified. Ultimately he received six honorary doctoral degrees, forty-five gold medals, three gold crowns, and, twice, the Nishan-i-Imtiaz, Pakistan's highest civilian award. He played his fame for what it was worth. This was the era when he began to buy houses and luxury cars, and to go around bestowing grants on hospitals, mosques, and schools. He shared his wisdom openly, on many public occasions. He sat on the governing boards of more than two dozen universities and institutes. He was personable, charming, and sometimes apparently humble—though in the way politicians can be, without being humble at all. When people visited him at his office, he gave them pictures of himself. When those people were reporters, he allowed them to fawn.

REPORTER: You seem to be very fond of learning different languages. In fact, you appear to be almost a linguist. In how many languages have you attained proficiency, and how? Any comments on this rather strange blend of being an exceptionally brilliant scientist and a linguist?

KHAN: I know a few languages. First of all, Urdu is my mother tongue. Then after the Partition I had to learn Hindi, which I still can read and write. Later on I learned some Persian. When I went to Europe, I learned German and Dutch. I know both languages quite well. While in Europe I also took some lessons in French. And of course English has been my second language all these years. I wish I could learn Russian and Chinese, but I couldn't find the time.

REPORTER: Do you have any hobbies, and how do you relax after a strenuous day?

KHAN: I used to go fishing, fly kites, and play hockey in my young days. Then I played volleyball at university. Now it is so difficult to do these things. I do some walking and play with our dogs and cats. It is very relaxing. I also read quite a bit. We go to bed very late, usually after midnight, as my wife is also always doing something, knitting, reading, etc.

REPORTER: Thank you, Dr. A. Q. Khan.

Across two days in May of 1998 India broke a twenty-four-year hiatus and tested five atomic bombs. The largest of them was claimed to be a thermonuclear (fusion) device with a dialed-down yield of forty-three kilotons, roughly three times that of Hiroshima. A dialed-down yield is one that in war can be dialed up. After the test, independent analysts expressed skepticism about the stated size and nature of the explosions, but these were technical quibbles of little importance compared to the new political reality of an India that wanted to make such a show of its military power. Just a few weeks earlier Khan's laboratory had successfully fired its new intermediate-range missile (a North Korean derivative dubbed the Ghauri) on a maiden five-hundred-mile flight, and Khan had followed up with his typical saber rattling and bluster. Flown to its full thousand-mile range, his missile, carrying his bomb, could devastate Mumbai, Delhi, and a slew of other Indian cities, including Bhopal. The missile's flight does not, however, seem to have played heavily into the Indians' decision to test—in part because they disdained Khan as a loudmouth and buffoon. In fact, physical preparations in India had been under way for a month, and the decision to proceed was made for domestic political reasons by the insecure leaders of the governing Hindu nationalist party, the BJP, who wanted to impress the masses with their strength. Sure enough, after the tests there was widespread jubilation on the streets. The celebrants ignored the possibility that the next time a nuclear weapon was ignited in India, it might be dropping in from Pakistan and vaporizing them.

In Pakistan the Indian tests were seen as a direct and pointed threat. Special attention was paid to an overexcited Indian home minister named L. K. Advani, who declared that Islamabad would have to submit to this reality, particularly as it affected the dispute over the territory of Kashmir, and that Indian troops would henceforth chase Kashmiri insurgents in "hot pursuit" right back across the border into Pakistan. So much for the sobering effect of atomic bombs. As part of the package, the Indian press was full of taunts, challenging the Pakistanis to show, if they could, that their nuclear arsenal was anything more than a bluff. Either way the Indians figured to gain. If the Pakistanis did not now test a nuclear device, they would demonstrate their weakness, with delicious consequences for the local balance of power. If they did test, and successfully, they would join India as a target of international sanctions, but would suffer dispropor-tionately because of their greater dependence on the charity of the world.

The Pakistanis knew they were in a bind. They had weapons ready to go and had prepared a test site years before by boring a horizontal tunnel into the center of a desert mountain, in a re-mote district called Chagai, in the southwestern province of Baluchistan. However, they were getting clear warnings that if they answered India in kind, they would lose not merely direct American aid, which had slowly been increasing since the last cutoff, but also the large infusions of cash from other donor na-tions and international lending organizations that were keeping Pakistan's economy alive. A rare public debate broke out among Pakistani elites, during which a "peace faction" urged the coun-try's leaders to assume the moral high ground and let India take the heat alone. The soon-to-be-deposed prime minister, Nawaz Sharif, accepted repeated calls from Bill Clinton and Tony Blair, who urged the same. Sharif hoped for positive inducements— solid security guarantees and financial payoffs—and some were promised. Public sentiment, however, was overwhelmingly in fa-vor of a test, as was sentiment within the army—Pakistan's real center of power. After several weeks of hesitation the logic of the subcontinent prevailed, and Sharif decided to proceed.

On the night of May 27, 1998, just hours before the sched-uled test, word was received from Saudi intelligence that Israeli fighters, flying on behalf of India (of course), were inbound to take out Pakistan's nuclear facilities—specifically the laboratory at Kahuta and the test site in Chagai. Pakistan scrambled its own fighters and rolled its missiles out of their shelters in preparation to launch. Months later Khan gave an interview in which he was alleged to have said that at Kahuta that night nuclear warheads

were loaded into the Ghauris—a statement he subsequently denied, and which for technical reasons seems dubious. In any case,
the Indians responded immediately by preparing their own aircraft and missiles, and for a few hours the countries came close
to a nuclear exchange.

Had this occurred, it would have been just the sort of non-
sensical war that people fear will result from the global spread
of nuclear weapons to countries like Pakistan—places with insecure political and military institutions, primitive command-and-
control systems, inadequate information sources, and ultrashort
windows for response to their nuclear neighbors. It seems especially significant, therefore, that on the night of May 27, 1998,
the leaders of Pakistan had the sense to hesitate and pick up their
phones. The United States and other nations assured them that
they were safe, the Israeli attack never materialized, and May 28
dawned normally for the residents of the great cities on both
sides of the border.

That same afternoon a small group of Pakistanis associated
with the weapons program, including, of course, A. Q. Khan,
gathered in a concrete bunker in Chagai, facing the chosen
mountain seven miles away. Pakistan later reported that five nuclear bombs had been placed inside the test tunnel where it
hooked sharply, eight hundred feet beneath the mountain's peak.
The bombs were fission devices, based on either the Kahuta or
the PAEC's design, or both, and containing highly enriched uranium—though a remote possibility exists that a plutonium device
was among those tested. The details remain secret. One bomb
was said to be large, and four to be small. They were wired to
detonate simultaneously—a practical arrangement that has, however, led to endless disputes about how many were actually in-

volved. The official number of five was intended to equal India's count—with the special surprise of a sixth bomb tested elsewhere two days later, to one-up the score. The tunnel was sealed with heavy concrete plugs. At 3:15 p.m. a PAEC technician directly under Samar Mubarakmand, the leader of the test site, pushed the button, saying, "Allah-o-Akbar"—God is great. After a delay of thirty-five seconds (during which, it is said, some observers prayed) the mountain heaved, shrouding itself in dust. The command post rocked. When the dust settled, the mountain's color had turned to white. In announcing the news Pakistan claimed a total yield that roughly equaled India's, of course. Independent analysts downgraded the actual yield by a factor of three—but so what? As far away as Cairo, Muslims danced in the streets.

After the test, Khan posed for pictures with the mountain behind him. He looked more subdued than pleased. It should have been his moment, the apogee of his life, and an occasion for the entire nation to praise his name. Khan-o-Akbar, people should have said; Islam has its bomb, and Pakistan is saved. Indeed, people did give him thanks, and over the next few years, by external appearance, he rose to new heights of glory and fame. But he was beginning to face serious troubles now—political forces that would ultimately lead to his arrest and disgrace—and a small but clear warning had been sent to him on that day. Control of the test had pointedly been awarded to the treacherous—no, traitorous—PAEC. Munir Ahmed Khan was seven years retired by then, but the institutional rivalry had not eased. Now this Samar Mubarakmand—a PAEC flunky, a carpetbagger, a twit—had been parachuted in to lead the site. It was Mubarakmand who had been given the honor of orchestrating the event. And Khan had been allowed to visit as a "courtesy."

This treatment continued after Khan flew back to Islamabad. There was no official delegation to greet him. That welcome was reserved for Mubarakmand, who arrived later and was met by the prime minister and a cheering crowd of hundreds. Khan was, in contrast, met by a small group of friends from the Kahuta plant, who waited for him in the "VVIP lounge," then drove with him to his house for tea with Henny. Khan looked haggard, perhaps because the near nuclear war had kept him up the night before, but more likely because of the frustrations of the day. Either way, he was not his normal irrepressible self. One of his companions at the tea recently told me that he had worriedly asked Khan what was wrong, and that Khan had not responded. It was a shock, he said, because for once Khan had seemed uncertain.

But looking back now, nearly a decade later, the answer can be known. In Pakistan people perceive more than they need to admit out loud. There are cultural understandings about what goes on—houses on the shores of Rawalpindi's drinking supply. Pakistan had its bomb, and it was a good thing, but Khan's utility was almost over. He was a genuine patriot, much to be admired, but too strong for anyone's good anymore. Was he out of control? Not exactly: he was expanding the nuclear business around the world, but with the knowledge of others in the military and government. For the moment he just needed to be reminded of higher powers. It was 1998, and there was no thought yet that he would have to be destroyed.

FOUR

THE POINT OF NO RETURN

Beyond Pakistan, those aware of the full scale of A. Q. Khan's activities included a small number of nonproliferation specialists in the intelligence services of the West. These people, who were sworn to secrecy, were concerned by what they were learning, but they remained paralyzed so long as their own governments—and particularly the leaders of the United States— placed greater importance on propping up the various Pakistani regimes than on stopping the spread of nuclear weapons. Just outside these circles, however, stood a few unofficial observers who were harder to control, and who kept peering in. The most persistent of them was a highly specialized American journalist named Mark Hibbs, who is largely unknown to the public, but must rank as one of the greatest reporters at work in the world today.

Hibbs is a legend in the secretive realm of nuclear power. He is in his mid-fifties now, and is based in Bonn, Germany, where he lives with his girlfriend when he is not traveling. He travels a lot. With a slight shift in intent, he would have made an excellent spy. He looks like one, too, with a bearing so ordinary for a middle-aged man that from even a short distance away—in a hotel lobby, in a restaurant, on a European street—he can be hard to identify. His face would be ordinary, too, were it not for the exceptional intelligence that animates his features when he speaks, and his habit of frowning in deep concentration while reconstructing the events that have shaped his work.

Those events go way back. For more than twenty years, Hibbs has been reporting the news for *Nucleonics Week* and *NuclearFuel*, two publications with ultrahigh subscription rates and correspondingly low circulations, now disseminated primarily on the Web. These publications stand among sixty-five similar ones in a McGraw-Hill group called Platts, dedicated to the petro-chemical and energy industries. Other Platts titles include, for instance, *Megawatt Daily*, *Emissions Daily*, and *Dirty Tankerwire*. Subscribers to *Nucleonics Week* also receive daily "Nuclear News Flashes," which could be nicely shortened to "Nuclear Flashes," if only Platts would lighten up. But Platts will not. Platts is an un-usually profitable enterprise. Hibbs is its star, but earns just a modest middle-class salary that allows him to get by. Platts has a lock on him in part because there are so few journalistic outlets for his knowledge. Much of what he writes is of short-term inter-est at best, and only to regulators and nuclear-energy insiders; he has filed thousands of such service reports over the years. Em-bedded among them, however, are several hundred related dis-patches—usually inconclusive, yet accurate and precise—which together tell an ongoing story of consequence to the established order, and perhaps even to the survival of mankind. That story is about the gradual failure of Europe, China, and the United States to prevent nuclear arsenals from spreading around the globe, and of the ferocious determination to acquire such arsenals that postcolonial nations, some banding together, increasingly show.

It is to Hibbs's advantage that he is not, strictly speaking, a spy. Because he works in the open, without a security clearance, he is not bound by governmental policies and cannot easily be silenced. Some others outside government share his freedom—professors, analysts, and advocates—and a few of them are very good, but none have produced results to equal his. Superficially what he does seems simple enough: he ferrets out details from a wide variety of sources, fits them into patterns in his mind, and writes them up. But that requires unlimited patience, sound technical knowledge, an intense determination to avoid making mistakes, and a sense for the plausible in a world full of lies. These are rare attributes, and in Hibbs they combine. It helps that he is not a crusader, and that though privately he regrets the spread of nuclear weapons, his reports take no political sides. It helps as well that the publications he writes for do not accept advertisements and understand that their value to their readers lies in delivering the news, even if that news embarrasses the industry or is otherwise impolite.

He told me once that it is lonely work, more so even than ordinary writing, because for all his influence, he writes for an audience imbued with secrecy and therefore rarely hears from his readers. Speaking of a meeting he attended of the International Atomic Energy Agency, the IAEA, he said, "I remember I sat down in the back of the room, and there was a delegate from one of the Western countries who was sitting next to me. I looked at him, and on his lap he had a copy of an article I did on the Iranian centrifuge program. It was a Xerox of the article I did. And the copy was meticulously underlined, and some things were circled, and there were written comments in the margins. So I tapped him on the shoulder and said, 'You know, that's interesting. Can you tell me where you got that article?' He looked at me and said, 'Why do you want to know?' I said, 'Because I'm the author.' So what did he do? He turned white as a sheet and just ran out of the room! It was the weirdest thing."

Weird perhaps, but standard for Hibbs. That was his point. He said, "Sometimes I feel that what I do is happening in a black box. The readers have security clearances. They read what I write in classified rooms in government offices and companies all over the world, and often they don't like what they're seeing. So how do they react? They go and talk to their buddies, who also have security clearances. Or they send a message to their enemies, and it's the same thing. You could be unleashing a major international crisis and wouldn't even know it, because it's all secret. Once the information is out there, you have no idea what's going on. Most of the time you just don't know. You don't hear about it. The reaction itself becomes classified. The lack of feedback is the really disturbing thing about this job."

Still, as he admitted to me, he has thrived.

It is not a life a person could seek or even imagine in advance. Hibbs was born in 1952 in a nondescript town in upstate New York. His father was a small-time accountant, and necessarily tidy. His mother was a housewife and came from a large working-class Irish family. Hibbs had six uncles and aunts from her side alone, and many of them lived nearby with children of their own. As one of the oldest among the cousins, Hibbs was a focus of the aunts and uncles' attention.

When the Vietnam War came along, they assumed that the right thing to do was to go off and fight. Hibbs went off to Cornell instead, and they were nonetheless proud. They believed that the purpose of attending a good university was to learn good manners—how to wear a suit, sip wine, and hold a knife and fork in just the correct style. For Hibbs it did not work out that way. He joined the rebellion of the time, and when he returned home on break, he ate with his fingers and flaunted his long hair. He opposed the war in Vietnam and wanted America to change. He marched in demonstrations. But he never became as radical as his friends. He simply could not follow along with other people's thinking without at some point considering that perhaps they were wrong. This of course was the real benefit of a good education, and it later served him well in deciphering the mysteries of nuclear proliferation. But even now in his family there must be some who do not understand.

In 1973, the last year of the draft, he graduated from Cornell with a degree in literature and history and drifted to Boston, where for some years he worked as a cartographer, designing maps for public-transportation agencies. In the early 1980s he moved to New York and enrolled in a master's program at Columbia to study diplomacy. He knew that Israel was nuclear-armed, and that India had tested its own device (the "Smiling Buddha" of 1974), but he was not aware of Pakistan's ongoing program to respond in kind. If he thought about nuclear weapons at all, it was in the conventional terms of the Cold War turning hot, and of global annihilation. In July 1981, the realities of proliferation were briefly thrust upon him, when the Israelis bombed the French-built Osirak reactor, in Iraq, ending a secret attempt by Saddam Hussein to extract plutonium from spent fuel, and to acquire a nuclear arsenal of his own. But Hibbs did not imagine that he himself would ever be involved in such matters.

He had a talent for language, which allowed him to learn German and eventually Dutch, French, some Russian, and a little Chinese. After leaving Columbia, he stayed on in New York, working as a freelance consultant and editor, primarily for a German government office, but he found it difficult to earn a living and so left for Europe, from which he has never permanently returned. For a while he lived in London, doing research for the *Financial Times* in the energy business—an area previously unknown to him, but of sufficient depth to engage his mind. He moved to Bonn, where he continued the same work, and contributed occasionally to *BusinessWeek*. His writing was concise. He was in no sense yet anything like a spy. But without having thought his career through in advance, he had become a reporter.

In 1986, when Hibbs was thirty-four, the Soviet reactor at Chernobyl, in Ukraine, melted down. Hibbs began to travel to the Soviet Union to report on the nuclear industry there, a subject still largely hidden from view. He was fascinated by the puzzle it presented. He was a fast learner, capable both of grasping physical technicalities, and, more important, of navigating the complex political terrain that surrounds the use of nuclear power. His interest in the field expanded worldwide. By then he had found his outlet, too, and was writing for Platts, which soon hired him full-time.

For a while he wrote only about civil nuclear power, filing such dispatches as "DWK Chooses Bavarian Site for First Big German Reprocessing Unit" (*Nucleonics Week*, February 7, 1985, 348 words). For anyone outside the industry, it was mind-numbing stuff. But beneath the surface of nuclear technology in Europe was action of a different sort: all the companies eagerly doing business with the growing number of nuclear-weapons aspirants. Much of the business that Hibbs uncovered was questionable but not obviously illegal. Then as now, European attitudes were soft, despite official abhorrence of such activities, because in private the nuclear-nonproliferation initiatives— accompanied as they were by repeated U.S. scolding—were perceived by many European officials as yet another self-serving American crusade. Along with their resentment of American domination came an understanding that providing nuclear-energy technology (especially in big packages to the Middle East) was a way of gaining European influence in important regions. Hibbs began to write extensively about the activity in 1988, when the German parliament, the Bundestag, finally opened an investigation. For two years government officials and businessmen were called in to explain their dealings, especially with Pakistan. Some sessions were tense. In the end, however, the Bundestag issued a report absolving German companies of involvement in the trade. It was absurd. Hibbs wrote up the Bundestag's report at length but essentially brushed it aside as a whitewash.

Neither he nor his readers needed the Bundestag to tell them what was going on. Pakistan's nuclear-weapons program, though officially denied, was well known to the world by then, as was the existence of its shadowy procurement network in Europe. A. Q. Khan, from his laboratory in Kahuta, had been bragging about it for years. Indeed Khan was already such a figure in the West that as far back as 1985 he had been featured in *Time* magazine. In the European and American press Khan was portrayed as an evil scientist and a treacherous spy, but at this late stage in history in many ways it made sense for Pakistan to have the bomb—as it did for all the other nuclear aspirants, and for the established powers including the United States. In private Hibbs would probably have disagreed; recently to me he characterized Khan's efforts as "diabolical." But for the most part he kept those thoughts to himself and in print went hard after the nuclear news.

Some of that news continued to be of Pakistan. A few of the most blatant suppliers were prosecuted in Germany, the United States, and Switzerland; more were identified, but for lack of proof of intent, they were left to continue the trade. The Pakistani procurement network remained large and robust, providing not only for A. Q. Khan's uranium-enrichment plant, but also for the rival plutonium program at the PAEC. But other aspirants now were involved as well. The Berlin Wall fell, the Cold War ended, and the trade in nuclear technology grew. Hibbs by then was an expert, and the one reporter everyone read. Over the 1990s he dug through the evidence of illicit trades, forming hypotheses in his mind, and asking increasingly precise questions to obscure specialists who knew of him but did not necessarily know what he was after.

I asked him to take me inside his investigative process. He said, "There was a German company that was exporting a certain device to Pakistan that in the worst case could have been for the nuclear-weapons program. All the surface evidence suggested that, no, this was the case of a scientist who went to Pakistan and sold some equipment to an innocuous research institution—and that was the end of it. That was the official explanation in Germany. But then I looked at it, and looked at it again from a couple of different points of view, and there was a very small chance that the equipment could have been used for removing tritium, a gas that comes into play in nuclear weapons. I wondered, could you use the equipment for that? I mean it's pretty far-fetched, but is it possible? After a while I realized you *could* use it for that. Then I wondered, is there anything else he did that indicated he had the know-how? I started talking to people and just kept asking one question after another. I was operating in a vacuum, and people in the nuclear laboratories in the U.S. weren't supposed to be telling me anything. But I kept asking, could it be this, and could it be that, and if that's true, could it also be this? And after several months when it appeared that the answers were all yes, finally the article I wrote stated that this guy in Germany had exported equipment to Pakistan for the removal of tritium. And I'm told that inside the U.S. laboratories there was a shit storm, because what I wrote matched what they were thinking, and it was all classified."

I said, "But day to day, what does that work really look like, tangibly?"

He said, "It looks like talking to as many people as you can."

"With narrow questions?"

"Yeah, but also general, generic questions. If you call somebody in a government laboratory, and you ask him, 'Do you think this German is exporting equipment for Pakistan's nuclear-weapons program?' the guy will probably hang up. He'll think, 'What? Nuclear weapons in Pakistan? This is a government laboratory, and this reporter doesn't have a security clearance! *Get OFF the phone.*' But if you meet the same guy at a conference, and you ask him a generic question about the configuration of the machine—'If the piece of equipment is configured like this, could it be used for that, could it be used for this?'—then maybe he will answer. And then if you ask a bunch of different people the same generic question, maybe something will crystallize out of it, and you'll get closer."

Hibbs got so close that he kept hitting the mark. He was the must-read, the spy's spy, a one-man intelligence service at bargain prices. The dispatches he filed were so short and technical that for general readers they could be difficult to decipher. Sometimes he seemed to be describing mere wisps of smoke. But by 1989 the smoke was rising on multiple horizons. Word emerged through Israeli intelligence that Saddam Hussein, having suffered the loss of his Osirak reactor, had reconstituted a nuclear-weapons program and was pushing to build a functioning bomb, which he would have within two years. Iraq had signed the Non-Proliferation Treaty and had therefore been subject to twice-yearly inspections by the UN's International Atomic Energy Agency, the IAEA. Such inspections were at that time strangely unobtrusive, worldwide. They occurred by formal invitation, with itineraries controlled by the host governments and negotiated weeks in advance. In Iraq they had resulted in some good dinners and belly-dancing shows, but nothing of nuclear note. By the IAEA's diplomatic standards, the country remained clean. This meant either that the report from Israel was dangerously false (and probably propagandistic), or that a serious failure had occurred at the very core of the NPT.

After the Gulf War it turned out that both were to some degree true—but that was in the future. Meanwhile, after the Israeli report came out, Hibbs filed an initial dispatch, the first of more than 160 that he wrote on nuclear proliferation in Iraq, in which he described widespread skepticism among technicians that any Iraqi program could be so close to producing a bomb. His article was a call for caution. In time his skepticism of the Israeli report became a point of contention with the mainstream American press, which reflected the U.S. government's now notorious tendency to take Saddam at his word, and to exaggerate the immediate nuclear dangers that he posed. Hibbs reflected a more sober view. His writing was based on the closest attention to detail. He did not doubt that Iraqi engineers could someday build a bomb, and that Saddam Hussein was possibly the man to use it, but he was aware of the technical difficulties that would first have to be overcome.

As usual, the largest difficulty was the acquisition of sufficient quantities of bomb-grade fuel. Years later, it became known that the Israeli report, though far too alarmist, was not entirely off. Iraq was indeed engaged in a nuclear-weapons program. It had abandoned the hope of extracting plutonium from its civil reactors, and like Pakistan, it had instead decided to pursue weapons built around cores of highly enriched uranium. As a signatory to the Non-Proliferation Treaty, it had the right to use lower-grade enriched uranium for power generation and research, but because such fuel was monitored by the IAEA, it was difficult to divert into a weapons program without attracting attention. The solution was to construct an entirely separate enrichment program that from start to finish would remain hidden from sight, or at least deniable. In the mid-1980s—toward the end of Iraq's war with Iran, when Saddam was still something of a friend of the United States—Iraq launched a secret initiative to buy or steal the necessary equipment, mostly from private companies in the West. Even while expressing skepticism about the conclusions of the Israeli report, Hibbs was the man who eventually caught on. Writing from Bonn in the summer of 1990, just after Iraq's invasion of Kuwait, he broke the news of an extensive Iraqi procure-

ment effort in Europe and the United States, whose purpose was
to acquire the components necessary for a uranium-enrichment
centrifuge plant.

Here at length is Hibbs in full stride, and, for general readers,
less demanding than at other times:

NuclearFuel

August 20, 1990

Customs Officials Say Iraq Is Shopping for Centrifuge U Enrichment Hardware

By Mark Hibbs, Bonn

*Iraq is actively seeking technology for development of an
unsafeguarded gas centrifuge complex, nonproliferation
experts, diplomatic sources, and customs officials said this
week.*

*Until now, most experts have assumed that Iraq has
not been making a focused attempt to acquire centrifuge
technology. "Iraq is not Pakistan," one U.S. government
official said. However, said Leonard Spector, a senior asso-
ciate at the Carnegie Endowment for International Peace
in Washington, D.C., information now coming to light
"suggests that Iraq has a list and is going shopping."*

*In the latest case to come to light, NuclearFuel has
learned that Swiss authorities are investigating companies
which may have sent end caps for centrifuge tubes to Iraq
under contract from a German company which exported
centrifuge-related equipment to Iraq in 1988 . . .*

Iraqi president Saddam Hussein has reiterated his

willingness to acquire nuclear weapons, a step which would violate Article II of the Nuclear Nonproliferation Treaty (NPT), signed by Iraq in 1970. Diplomatic sources are now questioning the credibility of Iraq's NPT commitment.

Investigative sources told NuclearFuel *last week that Swiss customs authorities are now investigating two Swiss firms' exports to Iraq. The sources would not name the companies. One of the firms is said to be a machine tool manufacturer, and the second firm, a metal processing specialist.*

The sources said these firms are suspected of having exported end caps for gas centrifuge pipes to Iraq. The end caps, experts said, are fitted onto the top and the bottom of each horizontal centrifuge pipe. The bottom end cap forms a perfect seal of the centrifuge pipe and has a needle projecting from the cap into the pipe. The top end cap contains a ring magnet and has penetrations for injection of UF_6 gas feedstock and for exit of enriched UF_6.

Like most centrifuge components, the end caps must be manufactured out of specific, high-performance materials to resist corrosion and mechanical stress, Western European centrifuge experts said. These sources said they believe that because end caps are "very useful for building centrifuges," their sale to a foreign party would require an export license in all Western countries.

Sources said Swiss authorities are investigating leads that the two firms worked under contract from the West German firm H&H Metalform GmbH. Officials at Bundesamt für Wirtschaft (BAW), West Germany's export control authority, told NuclearFuel *that company* sent flow-turn machines to Iraq in 1988, before these machines were included on Germany's list of dual-use technology requiring an export license (NW, 9 Aug., 2). Centrifuge experts said that flow-turn machines are used to cold-process maraging steel to make thin-walled parts in rocketry and in gas centrifuges. Should export of the flow-turn machines by H&H Metalform be linked to export of end caps by the Swiss firms, sources said, use of the flow-turn devices in centrifuge manufacture by Iraq would be "a very strong possibility."

In another recent case in West Germany, Export-Union GmbH, a Düsseldorf-based trading firm, has denied it assisted a clandestine effort by Iraq to enrich uranium. Three days before, West German customs police were tipped off that that firm sent centrifuge-grade maraging steel to Iraq. BAW officials said German customs will continue to investigate with the help of outside metallurgists.

Customs officials were tipped off about export of maraging steel to Iraq on August 10, after Iraqi commercial agents in Germany conducted quality checks on a shipment of specialty steel destined for Baghdad.

Maraging steels, which were expressly developed for rocketry and for manufacture of gas centrifuges, differ from conventional steels in that they are hardened by a metallurgical reaction that does not involve carbon. The term "maraging" derives from "martensite age hardening" and denotes age hardening of a low-carbon martensite matrix. According to German export regulations, such steel requires an export permit if its tensile strength is at least 1.7×10^9 newtons per square meter.

Export-Union officials have said that about 50 metric

tons of martensite hardened steel sent to Iraq earlier this year for a total of DM 3.8 million ($2.4 million) "couldn't have been used for the purpose of making ultra gas centrifuges."

According to Export-Union, that conclusion had been reached after the company itself, and officials from BAW, checked the materials specification of the steel to be exported and examined the end user. BAW informed Export-Union in writing on February 1 that "the material described in your export permit application does not require an export license."

The steel was manufactured by Saarstahl AG in Voelklingen, West Germany, and sold to Export-Union. Prior to export, materials experts at the Technischer Ueberwachungsverein (TUeV) Saarland checked the quality of the material against the specification on the export documents, to the satisfaction of Iraqi officials on hand during the inspection. TUeV was not required to report on whether the material could be used for making centrifuges or whether German export laws would be broken.

"We only checked to make sure the quality of the material matched the documents," a senior TUeV official said. "We didn't investigate what the steel was for."

European centrifuge experts said that experience has shown maraging steel is the best material currently available for centrifuge rotors, because output can be greatly increased and because maraging steel causes fewer corrosion problems than other materials.

Maraging steel is not absolutely necessary to manufacture gas centrifuges, however. "Its absence won't hold up Iraq if it really wants to manufacture centrifuges," one in-

dustry expert said. Early centrifuges installed by the tri-
lateral European enrichment consortium Urenco, for ex-
ample, were made of aluminum and fiberglass.

Iraq has also attempted to get centrifuge-related tech-
nology from the U.S., according to the U.S. Commerce De-
partment.

In March 1989, federal authorities seized 27 cases of
vacuum pumps about to be exported to Baghdad by the
firm CVC Products, Inc., Rochester, N.Y. The pumps, said
by CVC to be imported by Iraq for vegetable oil produc-
tion, were seized after Commerce determined they would
be "better used" to enrich uranium, according to David
Schuster, an official from the Office of Export Enforcement
in New York.

Hibbs did not stop there. Over the months that followed in
the fall of 1990, during Iraq's occupation of Kuwait, he continued
to dig into Iraq's European activities. Without drawing connections explicitly to Pakistan, he described a gray-market procurement network that was remarkably similar to A. Q. Khan's, and in
some cases exactly the same. The main suppliers were German,
with the Swiss and others helpfully pitching in. In December
1990, during the buildup to the Gulf War, the London *Sunday
Times* published an alarming report that seemed to corroborate
Israel's view and stated that Iraq's centrifuge program was merely
a year away from enriching enough uranium for a bomb. Hibbs
dug further and reported that the centrifuge in question was an
early Urenco design, not quite as advanced as the one presumed
to have been stolen by Khan, but perhaps good enough to do the
job—if it could be made to spin at the requisite speeds without
falling apart, then be linked to a minimum of several hundred

like-spinning clones in a cascade through which uranium converted to gas would flow.

The source for the centrifuge design was believed to be a German subcontractor to Urenco, whose engineers seem to have had access to the plans after leaving the company. Hibbs had traveled to Munich to meet one of the prime suspects, a centrifuge expert named Bruno Stimmler, who had gone to Baghdad as a consultant two years before, and against whom a German criminal investigation had been dropped in frustration. Hibbs got him to talk. Stimmler claimed to have no knowledge of Iraq's European source, but he admitted to having gone to Iraq to meet with Iraqi engineers, and he described in detail what he had seen of their centrifuge. He was so untroubled by the contacts he had made that he even told Hibbs about offering the Iraqis advice on modifications that would shorten the enrichment cycle. "But they were not interested," Hibbs reported that he said.

Hibbs himself was clearly reserving judgment. The Iraqis' lack of interest does seem unlikely, given the consequence of failure under Saddam Hussein, but Stimmler's measure of their program later turned out to be for the most part true. In brief, they had so far managed to build only a single centrifuge, which they had not fully tested. They must have made progress in the two years following, but according to Stimmler, as reported by Hibbs, the existence of a functioning centrifuge cascade in an operational enrichment plant, which was the premise of the report in the London *Sunday Times*, remained "completely far-fetched and absurd."

Then came the Western bombing campaign and the short Gulf War, during which Iraq was pushed out of Kuwait. As part of the peace settlement, new and more assertive nuclear inspections were imposed on the Iraqi regime. The inspections were carried out by the IAEA as usual, but also by a group created specifically for this purpose, the United Nations Special Commission, or UNSCOM, whose job was to search for weapons of mass destruction in all forms—chemical and biological, as well as nuclear. UNSCOM inspectors had the right to talk to whomever they pleased, and to go wherever they wanted without advance notice. The Iraqis obstructed them, of course, but over the next few years the inspectors uncovered a lot. What they found came as a shock. Though it was true that the Iraqi centrifuge program had never moved beyond the initial testing stages, it was larger and more serious than had previously been known. In intent, at least, this was not merely an experimental effort, but an industrial-scale attempt to build nuclear bombs. Furthermore Iraq had been pursuing an even larger program using electromagnet machines called calutrons—an enrichment technology declassified by the United States in 1949 and thought to be so obsolete that no one, including Hibbs, had suspected Iraq might choose it. In this case, however, "obsolete" meant easier to acquire. The calutron program had advanced significantly beyond the centrifuge efforts. In the summer of 1992 Hibbs reported that at the start of the Gulf War, Iraq had been about three years from producing enough highly enriched uranium to give Saddam his first atomic bomb.

But the greater shock was that such industrial-scale nuclear programs—using components acquired in the West, and directly under the nose of the IAEA—had gone largely undetected. Indeed, it became apparent that unlike other nuclear aspirants that had refused to join the Non-Proliferation Treaty (India, Israel, Pakistan, Argentina, and Brazil, among others), thereby exposing their intentions, Iraq had used the treaty as a cover, gaining greater freedom of action than it would otherwise have had. The

revelations emerging from Iraq provoked a crisis among nonproliferation specialists and diplomats; particularly in Europe and
the United States it was understood that if the diplomatic structures they had built were not to collapse, something would have
to be done. And something was—though within the conventional
framework, and as much in bureaucratic self-defense as in realistic hope of limiting the spread of atomic bombs. Over the years
that followed the Gulf War, the export-control lists were expanded, requiring a new level of governmental scrutiny (in participating states) prior to the export of "dual use" machines,
materials, and components. The export-control-list expansion
forced the European procurement networks largely underground by eliminating much of the ambiguity that had existed
until then, and requiring companies and consultants to break
their national laws if they wanted to pursue the nuclear-weapons
business, questions of conscience aside. In the new context of a
now demonstrated danger, some of the European resistance to
American activism faded away, and cooperation between the various intelligence and law-enforcement agencies improved. Furthermore in 1997 the Non-Proliferation Treaty was augmented
with an "Additional Protocol," allowing for more rigorous IAEA
scrutiny of declared nuclear facilities, if only in those countries
willing to join. There was a twist, which continues to limit the effectiveness of IAEA inspections today: as an international agency
whose primary purpose was to promote the civil use of nuclear
power, the IAEA was expressly prohibited from developing expertise in nuclear-weapons design. The prohibition was imposed
primarily by nationalists in the U.S. Congress, whose nightmares
included the metamorphosis of the United Nations into an independent nuclear-armed power. In practice it meant that the inspectors worked at a permanent disadvantage and could address

illicit programs only by auditing civil facilities for signs of deficits and diversions—exploring around the edges of the real question on everyone's mind. Nonetheless, the Additional Protocol, like the other measures taken in the aftermath of the Gulf War, probably did help to buy the world some time.

But even as the advanced nations closed ranks—essentially against the acquisition of nuclear weapons by poor and unstable nations—a new pattern emerged in which those nations began to help one another. There were reasons for this beyond convenience and greed. They amounted to a moralistic rejection of the discriminatory nuclear order as enshrined in the NPT. In principle the rejection made sense. If all peoples are created equal, why not especially in the possession of nuclear bombs? In more potent form, this was the same question that had until recently undermined export controls in Europe and elsewhere. The only possible answers were practical, but for certain countries they were no longer good enough. In any event this new form of proliferation lay largely beyond the conventional structures of control. As is now widely known, the pioneer was Pakistan, where A. Q. Khan exploited the connections he had developed in acquiring nuclear weapons and, by neatly diverting the inbound procurement flows, eventually set up a virtual nuclear-weapons market in which countries could buy the entire package, from the necessary machine shops and centrifuges to the blueprints for a bomb.

Without quite knowing what he was looking at, Mark Hibbs wrote about the early signs. In October 1990, in a report on the Iraqi centrifuge program, he expressed the skepticism among nuclear specialists that Iraq possessed the necessary engineering expertise to mount such an effort, and he mentioned the possibility of secret cooperation with Brazil or Pakistan—two countries beyond the IAEA's reach. It later turned out that those particular suspicions were unfounded—that the expertise for sale to Iraq was mostly German. But the possibility of nuclear collaboration directly between the poor was obviously on people's minds. In November of 1993 Hibbs broke the news that during a meeting the previous month in Baghdad, Saddam's deputy premier, Tariq Aziz, had told IAEA and UNSCOM inspectors that a Pakistani or Indian known simply as Malik and residing in Britain had in 1989 arranged for shipments of special high-strength steel for the construction of Iraq's clandestine centrifuges. Hibbs wrote that on the basis of this information British agents had tried to identify the man but had been unable to find him. At the end of his dispatch he mentioned that following the Baghdad meeting, the IAEA director, Hans Blix, had reported to UN secretary-general Boutros Boutros-Ghali that the information provided by Iraq appeared to be mostly complete, though there were still some gaps.

One year later, in 1994, Hibbs returned to the subject, writing that Malik was a Pakistani whose full name was Mazhar Malik and who lived in South London, where he had a small trading company, Development & Technology Enterprises, Ltd. The company appeared on a U.S. Department of Commerce list as having inquired into the export of food staples and cigarettes, among other materials. Hibbs reported that the high-strength steel had been sent by an Austrian firm through the port of Antwerp, Belgium, and had traveled aboard two Pakistani ships to Dubai before being trucked overland to Iraq. Because of lax Austrian export laws at the time, the British agents who had finally tracked Malik down concluded that nothing illegal had transpired, and the IAEA now considered the case closed. Hibbs had gotten through by phone, and Malik had denied knowing anything about the shipments of steel.

Then in the summer of 1995 the name came up again. Saddam's son-in-law Kamel Hassan, the man in charge of the prewar nuclear program, had fled to Jordan, and he was talking. Among the documents subsequently found on his chicken farm in Iraq was a secret memo written by agents of the Iraqi intelligence service, the Mukhabarat, and addressed to an unknown person in the nuclear-weapons program. The memo described an approach made to the Mukhabarat in Europe in October of 1990, during Iraq's occupation of Kuwait, by a Pakistani named Malik, who claimed to be an intermediary of A. Q. Khan's and offered to assist Iraq with the installation of centrifuges and the construction of a bomb. The asking price was $5 million up front, with an additional 10 percent commission to be paid on all materials and components obtained. In translation, the memo read:

> *Top Secret Proposal*
>
> *We have enclosed for you the following proposal from Pakistani scientist Dr. Abdul Qadeer Khan regarding the possibility of helping Iraq establish a project to enrich uranium and manufacture a nuclear weapon. The above-mentioned expressed it as follows:*
>
> *1. He is prepared to give us project designs for a nuclear bomb.*
>
> *2. Ensure any requirements or materials from Western European countries via a company he owns in Dubai.*
>
> *3. Request a preliminary technical meeting to consult on the documents that he will present to us. However, the current circumstances do not allow for an immediate meeting with the above-mentioned. There is the possibility*

*of an immediate meeting with the intermediary that we
have connections and good relations with in Greece.*

*4. The motive behind this proposal is gaining profits
for him and the intermediary.*

*5. The project has been given the code name of A-B to
use in correspondence and consultations.*

*Please review and give us your opinion on this matter,
so that we can take the initial steps to consult with him,
according to the notes and instructions that we received
from you.*

Thank you.

The Iraqis suspected that the offer might be a scam or a trap,
and they asked for a sample of the goods—possibly a component
or blueprints. They never received the sample, because the Gulf
War then erupted, and the ensuing international inspections
swept away any chance for such a deal. Nonetheless the offer was
almost certainly real. After the memo was discovered, Western
intelligence agencies and the IAEA kept word of it secret for
nearly a decade, until 2004, presumably because of political pressures, or to allow further information on Khan's activities to be
gathered. Neither Hibbs nor any other reporter wrote it up at
the time. But Hibbs was catching on to Khan and beginning to
piece together the signs that Pakistan's nuclear-procurement network had expanded into the business of spreading these weapons
around.

By 1990, when Malik approached the Iraqi regime, A. Q. Khan
was living flamboyantly in Islamabad—indulged by Pakistan's
military and civilian leaders, adored by the masses; ensconced in

a multitude of luxurious houses; surrounded by bodyguards and sycophants; writing checks to schools, charities, and mosques; lecturing; and continuing to lead the large government laboratory in nearby Kahuta that now bore his name. In addition to running the ten thousand centrifuges and producing the highly enriched uranium necessary for Pakistan's nuclear arsenal, the laboratory had diversified into the design and production of other weapons and was beginning to work on the problem of nuclear delivery, by means of ballistic missiles. Pakistan, which had not yet tested its warheads, continued officially to deny the existence of a nuclear-weapons program, but its denials were sly and patently insincere, like parodies of diplomatic sophistication, not intended to be believed. Particularly since the successful showdown with India three years earlier, during which Pakistan is believed to have threatened its Hindu neighbors with annihilation, Khan had been freed from the need to be discreet. In public he had assumed the role he believed he deserved—no longer just another refugee from the Partition, or an arriviste in a land of the poor, but, rather, of Khan the Magnificent, a "brilliant scientist" who was wise and progressive, and the savior of Pakistan.

The fame had unbalanced him. He was subjected to a degree of public acclaim rarely seen in the West—an extreme close to idol worship, which made him hungry for more. Money never seems to have been his obsession, but it did play a role. The nuclear laboratory was nourished by a large and secret budget for which no accounting was required and from which Khan freely drew funds as if they were his own. One might expect that Khan's largesse would have triggered investigations, but in Pakistan it did not. I have repeatedly asked people there if they ever wondered about the origins of Khan's wealth. One man close to the Musharraf regime tried to convince me that Khan's wife, Henny, came from a rich Dutch family, and that it was her money he was spending. But most people were straighter with me. They made it clear that my question was naive, and typical of an American abroad; they had not wondered about the origins of Khan's wealth because they had taken it as a given that he was skimming, like everyone else. A Pakistani parliamentarian made the point to me that some of the highest positions in the government today are held by people who are not merely corrupt and opportunistic but are the very icons of Pakistani criminality—people from families with a known history of murder, extortion, vote rigging, smuggling, and fraud. He had complained about this to Musharraf, who had advised him to be realistic: Pakistan, Musharraf had patiently explained, is an imperfect society. The parliamentarian shrugged. Even the army is run like a real estate racket, expropriating land from ordinary citizens, then passing it on to the officers for their personal gain. It is not by chance that Islamabad is a city of mansions, and that many of them are inhabited by retired generals. What was Khan's skimming compared with all that? And unlike the generals, who tended to lose every fight they provoked, Khan had at least delivered on his words.

Still, the idolization was excessive. I went to see another famous Pakistani who had received much of the same. He was Imran Khan, the Oxford-educated scion of a wealthy family who had captained the greatest-ever Pakistani cricket team, had led it to multiple victories over the Indians, and had in 1992 capped his athletic career with a World Cup. The subcontinent is so crazy for cricket that it essentially shuts down during important matches. Imran Khan, now fifty-three, is a tall and handsome man whose reputation for integrity—already strong—has been enhanced by his public denunciations of political corruption, and by his founding of a large cancer hospital for the poor in Lahore.

But that was not the point of my visit. Instead I wanted to talk to him about A. Q. Khan, and more generally about the nature of fame in Pakistan. I said, "It seems extreme. I understand how important the atomic bomb is to Pakistan. It is important to any country that acquires it. But I'm still wondering what is it about Pakistan that such a cult could be made around one man."

He said, "You have to understand the psyche of the subcontinent, and not just Pakistan. If you go to India, there is more idol worship there—the worshipping of 'stars'—than you will find anywhere else in the world. I was a Pakistani playing in India, but I've never had such adulation. I mean, in India everything is worshipped. They have idols for everything. Hinduism, you know."

"Okay."

"You will find Indian film stars—*all* of them—behaving like A. Q. Khan. It's not just the size of the crowds, it's their attitudes. Their film stars are like demigods, literally. Any celebrity. Their number-one batsman, for instance. The way he is treated in India is just incredible."

"People want to touch him?"

"More! He would need security. The first time we toured India, even to cross the lobby of the hotel from the lift to the coffee shop, we needed security guards. It was that sort of thing. The hotel was surrounded by thousands of people. We had never *seen* such a spectacle in our lives. And that culture is also in Pakistan—not to the same extent, because Islam challenges it—but don't forget that most people here were converts from Hinduism, and they have retained a lot of these qualities."

"And when you are on the receiving end? How do you keep perspective on yourself?"

He said, "People react so differently. I used to see on the

cricket team, boys coming up from poor backgrounds, and not well educated at all, and when fame would hit them, some would not be able to handle it. It would destroy them. For instance they would turn to alcohol. Because that is the trapping of success in Pakistan—it is very expensive to drink alcohol. So they would get into this crowd that would want to be associated with them: the nouveau riche, the old rich, they would invite these boys. A lot of the players would lose balance and think this was going to last forever. I think lack of education has a lot to do with it, because education allows you to stop living in a small world. What happens if you don't have an education and you get fame is that even in your own inner world you become oversized—this huge star."

"You studied history at Oxford?"

"And political science."

I said, "But A. Q. Khan was educated, too."

"Yes, so with A. Q. Khan I don't know. But when I was in England, I used to find that some people at the university who studied science, when they were outside their field, they were quite silly—stupid, really. Whereas people who went into the arts or general fields like politics or history, they were much better socially. I remember this one nuclear scientist who was on our team, and I would wonder how he was ever going to function in life. He did well on his exams, and he even got a first, which is very rare at Oxford. But beyond that?" Khan laughed at the memory. "I found Abdul Qadeer exactly the same. I remember we were once on a TV program together, in a panel of four or five people on a stage in front of a live audience of students. I heard him answering the questions, and I thought, 'This can't be the great Abdul Qadeer.' Because he sounded like a child, really. Someone in the audience stood up and said, 'You are so great, and I don't think you're getting the acknowledgment you deserve.' You know, he pandered to Abdul Qadeer. And instead of saying, 'Who in Pakistan has received more acknowledgment and fame?' Abdul Qadeer said, 'Yes, you're right. No one bothers about me in this country.' And he went on and on. I was so surprised. Here was this man, in front of these kids, and he was really feeling sorry for himself. It was bizarre. I thought, 'What is going on here?' "

The convenient answer to that question now, years later, is that A. Q. Khan was running amok, that he was an addict of sorts, unable anymore to find sufficient gratification from his activities in Pakistan, and that unbeknownst to either the Pakistani authorities or the American government he was going rogue, selling his nuclear secrets abroad.

There are elements of truth in all that, but only as there are in fiction. In Lahore I went to see a former finance minister, Dr. Mubashir Hassan, an engineer by training, who has in his later years become a pacifist, and one of the rare native critics of Pakistan's nuclear policies. Hassan is thin, with a gentle demeanor. On both days we met, at his ramshackle house in a leafy district of the city, he was dressed like a saint, entirely in white. We discussed the funding of Khan's laboratory over the years, and in general terms the extent to which Saudi Arabia and other countries had contributed to it. He said, "But if you want to find out exactly where the money came from, from what country, and in return for which state secrets and all that, or how the accounts were kept, how much was taken out by which crooks—all that will remain secret for a long time. There is really no way of knowing."

I asked him how Khan could have gotten away with so much

for so long. He said, "It is a cultural trait. The Western assumption that law should treat everyone the same way is no longer applicable in this country, in this culture. In Pakistan relationships exist only on an individual level, and as an individual, I am entitled to forgive you or penalize you no matter what the law says. It is a feudal culture—or a degenerated feudal culture. That is why there is no law for the elites in Pakistan, why they do whatever they want to do. So your question of why nobody investigated A. Q. Khan? He must have had allies in high places who ignored his activities. You've given us the bomb. All power to you."

But trading in nuclear-weapons technology is more than just a form of misbehavior. For better or worse, it implicates entire nations. To ignore such activities once they are known is in effect to participate in them. The lack of financial trails is inconvenient, but it does not obscure the essential history. A. Q. Khan had allies in high places who, rather than ignoring his activities, were directly involved and almost certainly approved. In Pakistan this can only mean the generals, including some of those currently in power, and to a certain but unknowable degree Musharraf himself. Hassan mentioned that they had certainly been given plenty of warning. Munir Ahmed Khan, chairman of the PAEC and A. Q. Khan's great rival, had been a longtime friend of Hassan's. In the late 1980s Munir Ahmed Khan had repeatedly complained to Hassan that A. Q. Khan was corrupt and, more important, that he was selling Pakistan's nuclear secrets abroad. According to Hassan, Munir Ahmed Khan had taken the same complaints to the generals in charge at the time, and of course nothing had been done.

Hassan used the term "traitorous" to characterize A. Q. Khan's activities. I said, "Can an activity be traitorous when the government itself is complicit, and in a country without effective law? I mean, at what point does such activity in such a place simply become a policy?"

He gave that to me. He said, "You're right. You can be a traitor only if the power is not aware."

But *policy* is probably too strong a word for what occurred. Pakistan's sale of nuclear-weapons technology abroad did not require a deliberative process, a chain of command, or a formal commitment to proceed. More likely it took the form of opportunities that occasionally arose, and that were acted upon by a small circle of friends—the country's military rulers, its co-opted politicians, and of course A. Q. Khan and his men. They knew that such activities would provoke the United States, Europe, and other great powers—but they did not think of themselves as bad people or believe that they were breaking international law. Whatever profits they hoped to gain from these deals would have been as much for the treasury as for their personal accounts— albeit in a country where such distinctions have little meaning. As to questions about the morality of spreading this technology around, they had some questions of their own—about the fairness of discriminatory nonproliferation treaties, and a world order in which the established nuclear powers keep trying to "disarm the disarmed." This was the emotional spillover from Pakistan's proud experience of building the bomb, and it fed a genuine sense of solidarity with all other nuclear aspirants, including even a potential antagonist such as Iran.

Indeed, Iran was Pakistan's longest-standing customer. In May 1991, Mark Hibbs reported in *Nucleonics Week* on the possibility that Iran had launched a secret uranium-enrichment program in pursuit of nuclear weapons, and that over the previous three years A. Q. Khan may have made several visits there. All this was officially denied. But soon after the article was published, Hibbs received a phone call from an American diplomat named Richard Kennedy, who at the time was the U.S. ambassador for nonproliferation and its chief representative to the IAEA.

Kennedy said, "I've read your last article."

Hibbs said, "Yeah?"

"You know that thing about A. Q. Khan—that maybe he went to Iran? Can you tell me who told you that?"

"No."

Kennedy said, "Can I assume it's a European intelligence source?"

"Yes."

"Will you tell me which government it is?"

"No," Hibbs said. "Does it strike your interest?"

Kennedy admitted that it did. "We have a very strong interest in Dr. Khan, and the Khan Research Laboratories. We pay very close attention to his work. In fact our interest in this man is so intense that you can assume if he takes a toilet break and goes to the john, we know about it. We know where he is."

Of course they knew, and how could they not? Everything Khan did was now larger-than-life. Though it would be politically inconvenient to admit this now, the United States was aware not only of Khan's peddling of nuclear wares to Iran, but also of the likely involvement of the army and government of Pakistan. Hibbs has reported that the U.S. ambassador to Islamabad from 1988 to 1991, Robert B. Oakley, went around the embassy fuming, "God damn it, they sold that stuff to those bastards!" and he believes that Oakley expressed the same emotion more politely at the National Security Council of the United States. Oakley, who now works at the National Defense University, in Washington, D.C., says that he does not recall knowing of the sales to Iran when he was ambassador, and that he was never asked to raise the matter with the Pakistani government. Oakley is still bound by his security clearances, and Hibbs believes he has been "whistled back" from talking. For political reasons more than for reasons of national security, these are some of the most closely held secrets in the United States. For the same reasons, the apparent lack of good information is pointed to as yet another U.S. intelligence failure (add it to the implosion of the Soviet Union, to 9/11, to Iraq), when in reality the CIA knew fairly well what was happening, and an awareness of Pakistani actions should count as a U.S. intelligence success.

Not that awareness required great skill: in Pakistan the intent to sell nuclear-weapons technology lay clearly in view. In 1989, for instance, the Khan Research Laboratories held the first international conference in what would be a fifteen-year series of occasional courses and symposia on issues pertaining to uranium enrichment and centrifuges. These meetings, which were widely advertised, amounted to barely disguised promotional affairs, clearly intended to demonstrate Pakistan's expertise to potential nuclear-weapons customers. By the end of the 1990s the Khan Research Laboratories were sending salesmen to international arms shows—in Malaysia, Indonesia, Abu Dhabi, and back home in Karachi—where they set up booths and passed out A. Q. Khan buttons and brochures advertising their conventional and nuclear products. In 2001 on the occasion of its twenty-fifth anniversary, KRL published a proud self-portrait, part of which read:

Keeping pace with the emerging demands of the competitive international defense products market, KRL ventured

*to offer its expertise, in the shape of services and products,
not only to the domestic consumers but also to an international audience of friendly countries . . . Although a fresh
entrant, the participation of KRL from Pakistan was
warmly welcomed. KRL has earned credibility not only in
South East Asia, but also in the Middle East and West
Asia. Its regular participation . . . has enabled the Laboratories to set up and maintain close cooperation in this vital
sector in many countries.*

Pakistan's Ministry of Commerce did its part, too. In July of
2000 it ran a full-page notice in the English-language Pakistani
press that advertised the nuclear-weapons products that Pakistan
had to offer—a full line of materials and devices that ended just
one step short of a ready-made bomb.

But back to Iran. In the late 1980s there were persistent
rumors of secret Pakistani-Iranian nuclear agreements, and as
noted, these were systematically denied. In 1991, however, Pakistan's army chief, General Aslam Beg, returned from a trip to
Tehran openly advocating the export of nuclear-weapons technology to Iran, and pointing to the several billion dollars of state
revenue that might be in the offing. He may even have written an
opinion piece in an Urdu-language newspaper expressing his enthusiasm for the idea—though in Pakistan recently he denied
this to me, and I was unable to track the piece down. Beg is an
anti-American, with sympathies for Iran, and he says that he is
the target of a Jewish conspiracy of lies. Be that as it may, he was
told to keep quiet in the early 1990s, not because his ideas were
controversial, but presumably because the transfer of blueprints
and centrifuges was already under way.

Hibbs was onto it fast. In November 1991, having previously

written about the unconfirmed visits of A. Q. Khan, he described an unnamed Western government's suspicion that Iran had obtained uranium-enrichment technology from Pakistan, and that this technology appeared to be that of Urenco, the consortium from which Khan had stolen designs. The official reaction in Europe and the United States was "no comment." This was to remain a secret world beyond view of the public. Hibbs was left to pursue his work alone in his black box.

Unbeknownst to him, in the 1990s the CIA concluded that the Pakistan-Iran connection had cooled, in part because the centrifuges that Pakistan had sold were castoffs, prone to vibration, and inefficient compared to more modern designs. As a result, U.S. interest in Khan diminished, and to some extent the trail was allowed to grow cold. Hindsight shows that this was a mistake: Khan remained as ambitious as ever, and like any good vendor, he offered improvements to his client. His relations with Iran remained strong, and all the better because they were out of sight. Throughout that decade, however, as Hibbs occasionally reported, U.S. suspicions remained strong that Iran continued to pursue a nuclear-weapons program—with the perhaps unwitting aid of Russia and China, both of which were eager to sell civil nuclear technology to Iran, as they are today.

In 2002, a glimmer of light illuminated Hibbs's black box: a confidential source at the IAEA alerted him that Iran had proceeded so far with a centrifuge program that it was ready to open a production-scale enrichment plant. Hibbs asked if the IAEA had any information on the origin of the design.

His source said, "It's indigenous."

Hibbs didn't believe it. He said, "There's nothing indigenous about a centrifuge program in Iran. There's nothing remotely indigenous about it. It's stolen. Believe me, it's *got* to be stolen."

Stolen or purchased. Hibbs studied the question, and with
the shreds of information he had, he painstakingly formed a picture in his mind. He asked himself, How powerful is this machine? How big is it? How much uranium could it conceivably
enrich? How fast? And how long has it taken the Iranians to develop it? He went back to his notes of a decade before and read
all his old files and finally concluded that it had to be a Urenco
design and probably from A. Q. Khan. But Hibbs needed some
sort of confirmation. With the evidence in hand, he went to see a
confidential source from a U.S. agency, in Washington, D.C.
They met in a coffee shop. Hibbs is diffident by nature, but he
got right to the point: "Does the U.S. government know where
the technology came from?"

His source did not answer right away. Apparently he had not
anticipated this question, and he needed time to decide how far
to go. The choice was between "no comment" and telling the
truth, because only a fool would lie to Mark Hibbs. The man
paused for a long while. Finally he said, "Yeah."

Hibbs said, "Where did Iran get it from?"

Again the man paused. "Well, it's the same . . . " He stopped
himself. Earlier that year the United States had leaked word that
North Korea had received prototype centrifuges from Pakistan in
return for missile technology—in a state-to-state swap. The leak
was not directed against Pakistan, but against North Korea,
which was accelerating its nuclear-weapons programs and would
soon withdraw from the Non-Proliferation Treaty. In any case,
Hibbs's contact decided to go ahead. He said, "There's only one
country that's exporting centrifuge technology."

"Do you mean Pakistan?"

"Yeah."

Hibbs said, "You realize, if I trust you on this, and flesh this out, and write it, there's going to be a shit storm, and basically it's going to be denied everywhere."

"Yeah."

Hibbs wrote it up, and in January 2003 his editor put it on page one of *NuclearFuel*, under the drab Platts-style headline "Pakistan Believed to Be Design Data Source for Centrifuges to Be Built by Iran." It was the most important work of Hibbs's career to date—a 2,164-word masterpiece that went to the center of Pakistan's activities and with unerring precision mapped the recent history of nuclear proliferation. The reaction, as Hibbs had predicted, amounted to a chorus of official denials—with various professors chiming in to explain why, for cultural or historical reasons, Pakistan would never have helped the Iranians to arm. Was Hibbs aware, for instance, that the two countries had supported opposing factions in the Afghan war? But Hibbs stood his ground.

Later he said to me, "There was no comment from the IAEA. I continued to interact with the sources of that story. Throughout 2003 they kept telling me, 'You're not only warm and hot, but the IAEA is very angry that you are not letting them control the flow of information. They're onto Pakistan. They know that individuals in Pakistan were deeply implicated in this program. But they can't use the P-word. No one will say, "Pakistan." It's all being discreetly negotiated between the IAEA, the United States, and other countries.'" The problem for the United States was that Pakistan was again a trusted ally, this time in the effort to dismantle Al Qaeda.

I said, "So they wanted you to pipe down."

Hibbs said, "Anyway we kept working on Pakistan, and more and more bits of the story got confirmed. I kept fingering Pakistan, fingering Pakistan, and pissing off the IAEA and the U.S.

government, because at that time they were saying, 'We want to make a deal with these people. We want to make sure it doesn't get out of control.' "

I said, "The story or the activity?"

"The story. They wanted to control it."

Controlling a story once Hibbs starts into it is not an easy trick, particularly because of the dedicated nonproliferationists within the ranks of government, who refuse to submit to higher political agendas and are sometimes therefore willing to talk. The Bush administration did manage to engineer a partial shelter for Pervez Musharraf, allowing him on behalf of the United States to pursue his "war on terrorism," largely against his own people, along the border with Afghanistan. Nonetheless, across the months of 2003, as revelation led to revelation, it became obvious that A. Q. Khan's nuclear empire, which had long been penetrated yet neglected by the West, was at last starting to fall apart.

The trouble over North Korea served as an early warning to Khan—or it could have, had he been wiser and less enamored of himself. Cooperation with the North Koreans dated back to 1992, when Pakistan, having acquired nuclear weapons, cast around for a missile design capable of carrying them. Groups of Pakistani engineers and officials made several trips to North Korea to witness test flights of a promising medium-range missile called the Nodong. They later struck a deal. Over the decade, North Korea provided Pakistan with missile prototypes, which were modified and produced at the Khan Research Laboratories, resulting in the successful Pakistani flight just before the tit-for-tat nuclear tests of India and Pakistan in 1998. In return for the missiles Pakistan provided the North Koreans with centrifuge

prototypes—the same old Urenco design—and gave them uranium enrichment and procurement advice. This was particularly
important, because North Korea had been pressured into suspending its plutonium-extraction programs, but, having withdrawn from the Non-Proliferation Treaty, was under no explicit
obligation to desist from the alternative path to nuclear
weapons—the refining of highly enriched uranium. The North
Korean deal with Pakistan was secret, of course, but Western intelligence services found out. Behind closed doors in 2000, U.S.
officials confronted the Musharraf regime with what they
thought was irrefutable evidence (much of it photographic) of
the North Korean centrifuge trade. The Pakistanis categorically
denied that any such activity had taken place. They looked the
Americans in the eye and lied, and they did not care that the
Americans knew it. The transfers continued. The Americans per-
sisted, some believing that bombs in the hands of Pyongyang
would be more dangerous even than bombs in the hands of
Baghdad or Tehran. Eventually Musharraf came up with a convenient answer: while admitting to no wrongdoing by Pakistan or
himself, or to any consummated transfers of nuclear technology,
he quietly pointed at Khan, essentially for being out of control.

His pointing took the form of a mock investigation. Khan was
making frequent trips to the Gulf city-state of Dubai, where like
many rich Pakistanis he owned a home, and where increasingly
he sought medical care for himself and his wife. Dubai had long
served as an offshore transshipment hub for the Pakistani nuclear-
procurement network, and it served just as well now as a center
for the business of nuclear distribution. Khan's main collaborator
there was a young Sri Lankan named Buhary Syed Abu Tahir—a
wholesaler of consumer goods who had warehouses full of televi-
sions and personal computers, and who had supplied air condi-

tioners to the Khan Research Laboratories before gradually getting involved in the smuggling of nuclear materials. Tahir seems
to have been a morally neutral character, friendly to Khan and
sympathetic to the aspirations of developing nuclear powers, but
motivated primarily by the money to be made as a middleman.
Khan did not begrudge him his profits and had indeed grown so
fond of Tahir that he teased him about his love life and sometimes treated him like a son. But Khan himself remained the
great moralist—not averse to personal gain, and delighted to
wheel and deal in luxury in Dubai, but convinced that whatever
he did, he did for Pakistan.

Khan was dumbfounded therefore, upon return from a short
trip to Dubai in the spring of 2001, when Musharraf, having
called him in for a conversation, told him that he had been under
surveillance by Pakistani agents, and that there were concerns
about financial improprieties. Improprieties? In the world of
Khan the word had lost any meaning. There was no question of
going to prison, but in early 2001, just a few days short of his
sixty-fifth birthday, A. Q. Khan was gently relieved of his command, forced to retire with honors from his cherished laboratory,
and "promoted" to the position of scientific adviser to Musharraf.
This last was a particularly nice touch.

There is evidence that the exchanges with North Korea continued for at least another year. When finally the Bush administration decided to go public with its concerns about the North
Koreans' nuclear-weapons program, it delayed leaking the intelligence information until late October of 2002, after Congress had
given its approval for the U.S. invasion of Iraq. It later turned
out that the North Korean centrifuge program was merely a fall-
back: the regime in Pyongyang had continued on the path to an
implosion-style plutonium bomb, one of which it finally tested

(with limited success) in October 2006. Nonetheless the blundering in the fall of 2002 defies belief: while dragging the United States into a disastrous war in the pursuit of phantom weapons programs in Iraq, the U.S. government condoned the tangible actions of Pakistan—which, as any reader of Hibbs would have known, was delivering nuclear-weapons capabilities into the hands of America's most significant enemies, including regimes with overt connections to Islamic terrorists. Before the attacks on New York and Washington, Musharraf himself had accommodated Osama bin Laden, had openly supported the Taliban, and had used international jihadists against the Indians in Kashmir and beyond. But times had changed, and by October of 2002 Musharraf was Washington's friend, trying to suppress the Islamist idea by gunning it down—even if at the same time his intelligence services continued secretly to support the Taliban. With his move against Khan he had partially covered himself from the revelations of Pakistan's trade in nuclear technology. Secretary of State Colin Powell met with Musharraf, and afterward, when asked on ABC television about Pakistan's assistance to North Korea, said, "President Musharraf gave me his assurance, as he has previously, that Pakistan is not doing anything of that nature. The past is the past. I am more concerned about what is going on now. We have a new relationship with Pakistan."

The past was the past but it bore a striking resemblance to the present. Khan had been removed from the laboratories, but as the U.S. government must have known full well, he continued to run Pakistan's nuclear networks, and to pursue that business all over the world. Khan was very vulnerable now—a scapegoat positioned to take a fall—but he had become so stupid about himself that apparently he did not believe it, and in any case he was busy. Along with filling the import orders for Pakistan's ongoing nuclear-weapons programs, and arranging for the exports to Iran and North Korea, he was occupied with Libya as well. The Libyans had long desired nuclear arms, and like the Saudis they may have helped to underwrite Pakistan's original uranium-enrichment efforts, in the vague hope that Pakistan would produce a "Muslim" bomb to be shared. That didn't work out. But by the late 1990s, with Pakistan expressing its willingness to make deals, the terms were clear: solidarity aside, it was cash that counted, and foreign governments could simply buy the components necessary to become self-sustaining nuclear powers. Libya decided to proceed. Emissaries from Tripoli met with Khan and Tahir in Istanbul, and later in Casablanca and Dubai, to hash out the details. Libya is a primitive Saharan society, only a half step beyond the traditions of nomadic life, and less capable technologically than any other nuclear aspirant to date. Khan must have said to the Libyans that this did not matter—and given the record of the Europeans' earlier doubts about Pakistan's competence, he may have believed it. In any case he offered to equip Libya with a turnkey operation, including all the facilities necessary to enrich uranium, and ultimately to build bombs. The asking price was $100 million, which was a bargain for Libya, considering the international muscle that a nuclear arsenal would provide.

When Libya agreed, Khan turned as usual to his European suppliers; with their assistance, by 2000 he was installing dozens of centrifuges in a pilot plant on the outskirts of Tripoli. That same year he arranged for the delivery (either through North Korea or directly from Pakistan) of gasified uranium that, if fed in closed loops though the centrifuges, would eventually be sufficient to fuel perhaps a single atomic bomb. The gasified uranium was kept in storage and was apparently never used. This was a pattern throughout the program in Libya, which proved unable to absorb all the equipment that it had bought and left much of it lying unassembled in the shipping crates. Nonetheless Khan pushed forward on multiple fronts. The pilot plant was of course just the start. What Libya ultimately required was a sustained and efficient production line, involving ten thousand linked centrifuges, backed up by the ultraprecise computerized machine tools necessary to make replacement parts and an unending supply of bombs. The machine-tool installations were to be provided primarily by Khan's European suppliers, but with help from certain Turks known to him from the past. The centrifuges themselves were to be manufactured in pieces by various companies around the world, including at least one created solely for that purpose by Tahir and Khan.

In the first week of September 2001, six months after Khan's forced retirement in Pakistan, and several days before the terrorist attacks on the United States, the CIA issued a report that Libya had revived its nuclear-weapons program, and mentioned guardedly that such an effort required substantial assistance from abroad. It is known now that British intelligence was tracking the Libyans carefully, and it can be presumed that the CIA had not entirely forgotten about Khan. Three months later, in December of 2001, Tahir set up a shop southeast of Kuala Lumpur, Malaysia, to manufacture certain narrow-tolerance centrifuge parts for the Libyan contract. He called the place Scomi Precision Engineering. Created as the subsidiary of a company owned in large part by the Malaysian prime minister's son, it was overseen in part by Tahir's recently acquired wife, the daughter of a Malaysian diplomat. To manage the technical side, Tahir brought in a Swiss engineer named Urs Tinner—the son of a man alleged to have been a longtime supplier to Khan, Friedrich Tinner. It has been reported in Switzerland that Urs Tinner had been turned by the CIA, and that the parts he was producing for Tahir were intentionally faulty, but this runs counter to the official American assertions of U.S. ignorance and uninvolvement, and it has been impossible to verify. Either way, in December of 2002, centrifuge components began to arrive in Libya in large numbers.

Khan kept flying around, making deals and enjoying life. Among other more serious outings, he had taken to visiting Timbuktu, in Mali, where he would arrive in a chartered airplane with groups of his proliferationist friends, and where he funded the construction of a small hotel named the Hendrina Khan, after his wife. Apparently nothing nefarious was going on. In fact, the visits to Timbuktu were such grand fun that one of Khan's entourage wrote a book about them, containing such helpful advice as not to visit the Bamako zoo, and offering readers the privilege of accompanying the great man himself as he relaxed and toured about. But by 2003 such freedoms were coming to an end. With the IAEA having revealed the existence of secret centrifuges in Iran, and with Mark Hibbs standing on the sidelines repeatedly fingering Pakistan, the political pressures on Musharraf kept mounting.

For Khan the collapse came in the second half of 2003, as the result of a complex series of events. The problems started in June, when IAEA inspectors found traces of weapons-grade uranium on the surface of ancillary equipment in Iran. Iranian officials, who had been denying U.S. claims that Iran was pursuing nuclear weapons, were put in the awkward position of having to explain away the evidence: they admitted that the equipment was secondhand and said that it had been imported from another country. In August, IAEA inspectors found similar traces at another site, and the Iranians went further toward blaming Pakistan, without quite doing so by name.

Meanwhile Libya's leader, Muammar Qaddafi, who had decided to normalize relations with the West, was involved in secret talks with Great Britain and the United States about dismantling his programs of weapons of mass destruction. In October of 2003, apparently, the British and Americans decided to give him a push: they intercepted a ship called the *BBC China*, which was known to have left Dubai and passed through the Suez Canal carrying nuclear-weapons equipment destined for Libya. The intercept itself was a low-key affair: it amounted to a phone call to the ship's German owners, requesting that they divert their vessel to an Italian port for inspection. The request was backed up by the presence of a U.S. warship, but perhaps unnecessarily, since the ship's owners were innocent businessmen with nothing to hide. In Italy the inspection turned up five containers holding thousands of centrifuge parts manufactured by Scomi Precision Engineering in Malaysia (and packed in wooden crates boldly bearing the company's name), along with other components manufactured in Turkey, and paperwork showing that the transshipment through Dubai had been arranged by the enterprising Tahir. To the intelligence agents involved, none of this would have come as a surprise.

Nor would Khan have been surprised that Pakistan's operations had been penetrated. He had been working under that assumption for decades, without slowing down, and the loss of five containers, or even of the Scomi facility in Kuala Lumpur, would normally not have fazed him at all. But in a larger sense now he was losing control. In Libya the interception of the *BBC China* was seen as an inconvenient event because it amounted to being caught red-handed. It is necessary to discount the Bush administration's subsequent claim that Qaddafi was chastened by the invasion of Iraq, because by this time, in late 2003, the lack of Iraqi weapons of mass destruction was becoming a major public embarrassment, and the U.S. military in Iraq was clearly bogging down. Far from being impressed by Washington's resolve, Qaddafi was more likely invigorated by its blunder. Nonetheless he had decided to do business with the world, particularly with the nearby moralists of Europe, and soon after the *BBC China* seizure, he formally gave up on his nuclear-weapons program.

In November 2003 the Libyans accepted the arrival of IAEA inspectors and others, and began to answer questions about Libya's arrangement with Pakistan. The Libyans were more forthcoming than the Iranians had been. They provided dates, named names, opened their facilities, and eventually even allowed the equipment to be flown away, under IAEA control, to warehouses in the United States. Their centrifuges were mostly unassembled and incomplete, but they were of the same proven Urenco design as those in Iran—and similar to those being built now in North Korea. In December the news got out, with mention of the various cross-connections, and was published in the major American papers. How much worse could it get? In January 2004, having certainly made photocopies first, the Libyans handed over a bag from an Islamabad laundry containing the plans for a Chinese-designed implosion bomb, just like Pakistan's. On the margins were handwritten notes in English disparaging the hated Munir Ahmed Khan, of the PAEC. Clearly these plans had come from the Khan Research Laboratories, and possibly from A. Q. Khan himself.

Musharraf ducked into the same defensive position he had used before. He launched an official investigation and began hauling in Khan's staff for questioning. The conclusion was

known from the start: after nearly six years of warnings, beginning with the snubs Khan had received on the day of the test explosions in 1998 and continuing through his dismissal from the
laboratories in 2001, the time had finally come for Khan to disappear for good. Before checking out, however, he had one last
service to provide to the regime, and if he did it right, technically
speaking his life would be spared. On February 4, 2005, after
days of persuasion in Islamabad, he appeared on television and
absolved everyone but himself of blame. Speaking in English, a
language that relatively few Pakistanis understand, he said:

> *My dear ladies and gentlemen, as-salaam alaikum. It is
> with the deepest sense of sorrow, anguish, and regret that
> I have chosen to appear before you in order to atone for
> some of the anguish and pain that have been suffered by
> the people of Pakistan on account of the extremely unfor-
> tunate events of the last two months. I am aware of the vi-
> tal criticality of Pakistan's nuclear program to our national
> security and the national pride and emotion which it gen-
> erates in your heart. I am also conscious that any unto-
> ward event, incident, or threat to this national security
> draws the greatest concern in the nation's psyche. It is in
> this context that the recent international events and their
> fallout on Pakistan have traumatized the nation.*
>
> *I have much to answer for. The recent investigation
> was ordered with the government of Pakistan consequent
> to the disturbing disclosures and evidence by some coun-
> tries to international agencies relating to alleged prolifera-
> tion activities by certain Pakistanis and foreigners over the
> last two decades.*

The investigations have established that many of the reported activities did occur and these were inevitably initiated at my behest.

In my interviews with the concerned government officials I was confronted with the evidence and findings and I have voluntarily admitted that much of it is true and accurate.

My dear brothers and sisters, I have chosen to appear before you to offer my deepest regrets and unqualified apologies to a traumatized nation. I am aware of the high esteem, love, and affection in which you have held me for my services to national security, and I am grateful for all the awards and honor that have been bestowed upon me. However it pains me to realize in retrospect that my entire lifetime achievements of providing foolproof national security to my nation could have been placed in serious jeopardy on account of my activities which were based in good faith but on errors of judgment related to unauthorized proliferation activities.

I wish to place on record that those of my subordinates who have accepted their role in the affair were acting in good faith like me on my instructions.

I also wish to clarify that there was never ever any kind of authorization for these activities by the government.

I take full responsibility for my actions and seek your pardon.

I give an assurance, my dear brothers and sisters, such activities will never take place in the future.

I also appeal to all citizens of Pakistan in the supreme

national interest to refrain from any further speculations
and not to politicize this extremely sensitive issue of na-
tional security.

May Allah keep Pakistan safe and secure. Long live
Pakistan!

Khan then disappeared into his house, perhaps never to
resurface. The official Pakistani investigation continued, occasionally producing the news that yes, indeed, Khan had done
these things and was to blame. Several of Khan's staff members
were placed under house arrest as well. Outside Pakistan a few
additional actions were taken. Tahir was arrested in Malaysia,
though for the first nine months he was kept away from representatives of the IAEA. The Malaysians held an investigation and
eventually cleared themselves of any wrongdoing. Urs Tinner
was arrested in Germany and extradited to Switzerland, where
he was held in jail during an extended inquiry. Germany is trying
to prosecute one of Khan's alleged suppliers, and Holland is trying the same against another of Khan's longtime associates—but
both cases are in trouble. South Africa, which turns out to have
been an important supplier to the Libyans, is trying halfheartedly
to go after some of its own citizens. Meanwhile, Qaddafi has
been mumbling about having cut a bad deal, North Korea has exploded its first nuclear bomb, and Iran is rapidly arming despite
various diplomatic maneuvers that raise the possibility that it
might stop. As for the United States, it keeps repeating its exqui-
site claim to ignorance—that for all those years it knew practically nothing about the activities of A. Q. Khan.

But with or without the CIA, readers of Mark Hibbs have
long known what is going on. He is a disciplined reporter who
sticks closely to the news, but people with a sense for his beat—

this world of nuclear secrets—draw as much by reading between his lines. In September of 2005, for instance, under the headline "Pakistan Says Its Role in Probing Khan's Proliferation Is Finished," he led with two apparently simple sentences that are memorable as much for the questions they intentionally leave unanswered as for the statement of facts:

> *The Pakistan government said August 29 that its interrogation of Abdul Qadeer Khan, former head of the Khan Research Laboratories (KRL), about his involvement in proliferating Pakistan's nuclear technology abroad has been completed. "As far as we are concerned, I understand that whatever information that was there has been obtained and has been shared with the relevant countries, and [that] the relevant countries are satisfied with the information," Foreign Ministry spokesman Mohammad Naeem Khan told a weekly press briefing.*

The investigation was over? All available information had been obtained? It had been shared? With relevant countries? Which countries were they? Who chose them, anyway? And what about Khan? Since Musharraf had already pardoned him, and he had now confessed everything he knew, what was the reason for his continuing house arrest, and his ongoing isolation from Western intelligence and the press? Hibbs did not address these questions for the reason so obvious to his readers, that Pakistan's investigation was a cover-up and a sham—moreover of a sort only possible in a morally bankrupt and corrupt nation, where cowardly and illegitimate rulers, propped up by massive infusions of American dollars and dependent on their soldiers' guns, suppress genuine inquiries because they would be implicated themselves and, in the embarrassment that would follow, would be cut off from foreign aid, and driven from power by their own people, who almost universally now detest them. The problem for the United States, and conceivably for Europe, is that those doing the driving would likely be Islamists, who are growing in strength and numbers even within the military and intelligence services. The Iranians will probably beat them to it, but if Pakistani Islamists took power tomorrow, they would be the first Islamists with nuclear bombs. Hibbs trusted his readers to know all this and more when he wrote about the sham investigation's end. To me in Bonn he simply chuckled and said, "Ah, Pakistan."

But strictly in terms of nuclear proliferation, there is a question of what good a genuine investigation could do anyway—as Hibbs understands in full detail. There would be the immediate frustrations that Khan's network was spread around, that it operated in the gray areas of national laws, and that prosecutions would be undermined by political sympathies even if unambiguously illegal acts could be found. More difficult still, however, is the very nature of such a network, which is not a rigid structure that can be shattered and shut down, but something rather more like the Internet—a vast and informal web of infinitely flexible connections, capable of reshaping itself with ease, and concerned primarily with the flow of knowledge. Einstein and Oppenheimer predicted this years ago, when they warned that there are no secrets to protect: A. Q. Khan did not create his nuclear-weapons network so much as discover it as a condition of the modern world.

Such a world that has been equalized through the spread of nuclear weapons will pose complex dangers, but to the extent such complexities are related to the loosening of the alliances and guarantees that characterized the Cold War, the risk of an apocalypse may have been reduced. The desire for self-sufficiency, which will drive proliferation forward, is a measure of a new reality in which limited nuclear wars are possible, and the use of a few devices, though locally devastating, will not necessarily blossom into a global exchange. That is the flip side of proliferation, rarely addressed in public debate: the spread of nuclear weapons, even to such countries as North Korea and Iran, may not be as catastrophic as is generally believed and certainly does not meet the category of threat that can justify the suppression of civil liberties or the pursuit of preemptive wars. Furthermore, the evidence so far is that even the poorest or most ideological countries are subject to the conventional logic of deterrence and will hesitate to use their weapons because of the certainty of a crushing response—since they, too, have cities and infrastructures that they will lose. It is probably foolish to count on the larger stabilizing effect of mutually assured destruction, as some Pakistani apologists apparently do when they argue that war with India is now less likely than before. But it is a matter of record that nuclear weapons have thus far proved to be better political than military tools, and that not since their original spread from the United States has any national leader been able to make sense of firing them off.

The problem, of course, is that this deterrence may at any time fail.

Mubashir Hassan, the pacifist and former finance minister in Lahore, told me he worries that Pakistan, like the United States, is the sort of country that would actually use its atomic bombs. He said he had once asked Pakistan's leaders when they thought such use would be justified.

One said, "When we are threatened enough."

"But when will you be threatened enough? If India takes Lahore?"

"We don't know."

"But if you throw a bomb, and India throws two bombs back in return, what then?"

"So what?" the man said. "Then we die."

Hassan was appalled by this logic, but alternative strategies of "no first use" are credible only in the most richly endowed nuclear nations and are simply not realistic for countries like Pakistan. Once such a country has a bomb, it must be determined not just to use it, but to use it first.

In Islamabad I met a smart man close to the military who recognized that the risk of nuclear war increases with every successful act of proliferation, and that the danger is compounded in underdeveloped nations by poor command-and-control systems and fragile, overly bellicose governments. His attitude, however, was akin to a shrug: this is the world we live in, and so be it.

He said, "The best way to fight proliferation is to pursue global disarmament. Fine, great, sure—if you expect that to happen. But you cannot have a world order in which you have five or eight nuclear-weapons states on the one hand, and the rest of the international community on the other. There are many places like Pakistan, poor countries which have legitimate security concerns—every bit as legitimate as yours. And yet you ask them to address those concerns without nuclear weapons, while you have nuclear weapons *and* you have everything else? It is not a question of what is fair, or right or wrong. It is simply not going to work."

The man was right. A. Q. Khan proved it once, and then three times over again. There will be other Khans in the future. It

seems entirely possible that terrorist attacks can be thwarted—
though this would require nimble governmental action—but no
amount of maneuvering will keep determined nations from developing nuclear arsenals. North Korea, Iran, perhaps Turkey,
Egypt, Syria, Saudi Arabia, Brazil. Now and then a country may
be persuaded to abandon its nuclear program, but in the long
run, globally, such programs will proceed. Shifted to America,
and shed of its postcolonial indignation, the Pakistani's point becomes an argument not for standing down from the diplomacy of
nuclear nonproliferation, but for finding the courage in parallel
to accept the equalities of a maturing world in which many countries have acquired atomic bombs, and some may use them.

ACRONYMS

CBP	Customs and Border Protection Agency (U.S.)
CIA	Central Intelligence Agency (U.S.)
FAS	Federation of American Scientists (U.S.)
FDO	Fysisch-Dynamisch Onderzoek (centrifuge-engineering company) (Netherlands)
FSB	Federal Security Bureau (Russia)
HEU	Highly Enriched Uranium
IAEA	International Atomic Energy Agency (UN)
KRL	Khan Research Laboratories (Pakistan)
MPC&A	Material Protection Control & Accounting
NNSA	National Nuclear Security Administration (U.S.)
NPT	Nuclear Non-Proliferation Treaty
NTI	Nuclear Threat Initiative (U.S.)
PAEC	Pakistan Atomic Energy Commission
UNSCOM	United Nations Special Commission (Iraq)
Urenco	Uranium-enrichment company (Netherlands)